SECRET
NATURE
of the
Channel Shore

SECRET
NATURE
of the
Channel Shore

Andrew Cooper

BBC BOOKS

To:
Jeanne,
Julia and Charles.

Author's Acknowledgements

I owe a great debt of thanks to my colleagues in BBC Television for their support and skills during the making of *Secret Nature*. My special thanks go to Wyn Griffiths, Jenny Slater, Justin Smith, Rod Thomas, David Wells, Greg Wade, Phil Speight, Roy Roberts and everyone at BBC Plymouth. From BBC Bristol I must particularly thank John Prescott Thomas and Andrew Neal for their encouragement and support over the years. From London I thank Elizabeth Parker for the music and John Hale for skilfully mixing the tracks. For making the series possible I owe special thanks to John Kelly and BBC Enterprises.

Thanks are also due to those who made much of the photography possible: Roger Hosking and Brian Knox, whose own superb work also appears in this book, John Bowers, Nick Williams,

Heather Woodland, Nigel Smallbones and Norman Barns. The help and guidance I received from Ellis and Lyn Daw, Richard Weaving, Keith Chell, Chris Riley, Carl Farrell, John Waldon and Stan Davies made much of my work possible.

In the Channel Islands I owe a special debt to Frances le Sueur and the late Vic Mendham. Particular thanks must be given to the late Professor Leslie Harvey, Clare Harvey, Penny Rogers, Willie Wagstaff, Cyril Nicholls and the island's irrepressible boatmen.

I must thank Julian Ahearne and the staff of Newton Abbot Library for their research and to scientists and researchers Professor Alec Smith, Dr David Stradling and Dr Geoffrey Potts.

Thanks are also due to Sheila Ableman, Jennifer Fry, Frank Phillips, Grahame Dudley and particularly Deborah Taylor at BBC Books.

This book is published to accompany the
television series entitled Secret Nature

Published by BBC Books,
a division of BBC Enterprises Limited,
Woodlands, 80 Wood Lane
London W12 0TT

First Published in hardback 1992
(Published in paperback 1993)
© Andrew Cooper 1992

ISBN 0 563 20874 0 (hardback)
ISBN 0 563 36906 X (paperback)

Designed by Grahame Dudley Associates

All photographs by Andrew Cooper except:
Wyn Griffiths, page 25; Roger Hosking, pages 48 (bottom right),
124 (bottom), 152–3 and 182; Bryan Knox, Pages 79 and 86.

Set in Apollo by Ace Filmsetting Ltd, Frome, Somerset
Printed and bound in England by Clays Ltd, St Ives plc
Colour separation by Technik Ltd, Berkhamsted
Jacket printed by Belmont Press Ltd, Northampton

Contents

Introduction   6

CHAPTER ONE
Beyond Tide's Reach   11

CHAPTER TWO
Pure Lagoon   41

CHAPTER THREE
Turn of the Tide   67

CHAPTER FOUR
Life on the Edge   95

CHAPTER FIVE
The Channel Islands   131

CHAPTER SIX
The Isles of Scilly   165

CHAPTER SEVEN
Call of the Sea   201

Index   223

Introduction

The legendary lost land of Lyonesse is said to lie somewhere beyond the south-west of Britain, drowned by a rising sea. Yet it may not be as fanciful a story as it seems. If time could be condensed from centuries into seconds, much as the petals of a flower burst open on film, the birth of Britain as an island could be witnessed in a few minutes.

The foundations of the English Channel, its geological framework, formed gradually, but its final shaping was a quite different and perhaps even catastrophic event. The white cliffs of Dover and the facing chalk headlands in France are thought to be the ruined remains of a massive natural dam, a broad, chalk-faced ridge, resting on sandstone and clay, spanning the eastern end of the Channel and created by uplifting over the last twenty million years. When global temperatures plunged some three million years ago the most recent ice ages began. It was a period of extremes. The great freeze waxed and waned as the millennia passed – perhaps thirty-five times every 90 000 years or so. The advance of the ice caused sea levels worldwide to fall and the floor of the Channel dried each time. The returning warmth brought rising seas but the land bridge to Britain survived despite many floods. Wild animals crossed this way. So, too, did the first humans who ventured this far north, leaving little trace of their passing except, perhaps, footprints across the causeway.

Each time the immense ice sheets straddling northern Europe receded, the North Sea became a vast lake filled by meltwater and rain, stretching as far as Russia. Drainage from the glaciers into the Atlantic Ocean was hindered by the ice to the north and the ridge forming a dam to the south. The last warm spell of the ice ages occurred some 50 000 years ago and by then the chalk ridge was possibly weakened by the successive onslaught of freezing arctic conditions and intervening thaws. At this time the Channel floor lay up to 150 metres below the level of the lake. It was a situation that heralded disaster. Exactly when the dam was breached is not known but the evidence of its doing so is still to be found in the gigantic scars it left on the seabed. The scale was awesome. It may

St Ouen's Bay, Jersey. In the aftermath of the last ice age rising sea levels worldwide finally turned mere hilltops on the edge of a vast low-lying European plain into islands.

have begun as a simple overspill near the centre of the chalk ridge, but the force of the huge volume of water was so great that it tore away the rock surface, exploiting every weakness, until it burst through the dam sending plumes of spray skyward and shaking the ground. A steaming waterfall of Niagara proportions sent a wall of water hurtling down the Channel. Trees were uprooted and animals drowned in the flash of its destructive flood. Until then the biggest flow into the Channel had come from the gentle meanderings of the River Seine. The original breach in the dam was probably widened by the eventual returning flow of the sea. The process quickly gains ground. Even today the chalk cliffs that flank the Dover straits are retreating by as much as half a metre a year.

In the centuries following the end of the last ice age, around 11 000 years ago, the windswept tundra of southern England was very different from the warm and pleasant land of today. Then the view from the heights that now form the tall, south coast cliffs was of a vast, low-lying plain stretching into the continent. A few hills protruded from its margins while the central floor was cut by deep valleys with rivers flowing west. Within 3000 years only the Highlands of Scotland still had glaciers. Spring came earlier each year and melting ice poured from the mountains. Sea levels worldwide were rising fast. Ireland became an island and the Atlantic Ocean was driving a wedge between Britain and France. Herds of reindeer that had roamed this landscape akin to the present-day subarctic, followed the retreat of the ice northward. Plants and animals from the warmer south spread in their wake, gradually surviving further and further north. In time, a broadleaved band of hazel, wych-elm, oak and alder grew across southern Britain and mainland Europe, displacing the original forests of birch and pine as winters became less severe and summers lasted longer. The sea's encroachment of the land continued apace with storms speeding the process. Water flooded inland over low ground at a rate of perhaps up to 150 metres a year, advancing up the valleys, drowning the forests and heather-clad slopes. Hills dotting the lowland plain were transformed, turned into islands. The south-west of Britain became a peninsula and beyond its furthest tip a remote land mass remained high above the waves. Today, the Isles of Scilly are a fraction of their former size, but at that time another island, as large as Scilly although lacking its prominence, lay some distance to the north-west. Nowadays the plateau of Haig Fras lies 40 metres beneath the surface of the sea. Another island, however, survived a little longer. Around 8000 years ago, not far from the mainland cliffs of what we now know as Land's End, lay a land probably as lush, green and inviting as Scilly although its fate was already sealed.

To the east, two thousand years later, the last remains of the land bridge to the Continent had finally crumbled with the Atlantic surge. The tide swept away the debris and the familiar, narrow, chalk-lined straits were formed. Britain had become an island and the English Channel was born. At first the outline of the British coast was similar to that of the present day, but the sea level continued to rise another 2 metres before settling down again. During this time many river valleys and coastal plains were drowned. Offshore only the tallest hills and high plateaus survived the flood, while small islands succumbed to the sea. Over the centuries stories of lands lost to the sea have been told time and time again. Myths and legends rooted firmly in the distant past abound, although in time details are apt to be embellished. Some sea level rises may even be far more recent. Whatever the origin of the story, if you fly from Cornwall today, midway to the Isles of Scilly lie the jagged, wave-washed peaks of the Seven Stones reef. No one can be sure, but perhaps this is all that remains of the lost land of Lyonesse.

The English Channel is the busiest and best known seaway and its stormy waters have seen events that helped shape the modern world. There can be few places on earth where a change in the wind has altered the fate of a nation. Here it has happened more than once. In terms of human and wild lives these waters both unite and divide, forming a barrier to some, yet for others a highway and sustainer of life. A seabird's tour of the south coast reveals the diverse and dramatic nature of this coastline. Crossing from France, skimming the sea, brings the gleaming white cliffs of Dover into view – an enduring image of England. Westward lie more impressive chalk heights, a sheer rise of over 100 metres. The Seven Sisters reach out from Beachy Head and the ragged pinnacles of the Needles march from the Isle of Wight into the sea. Elsewhere along this coast the land slopes more gently to the shore, past Portland Bill, along the length of Chesil beach to the grey slumping cliffs of Lyme Regis. Further west still, past the open expanses of the Exe estuary and fine Dawlish sands, the red cliffs and limestone of Torbay and Berry Head, stretch the peaceful waters of Slapton Ley. Westward still, the shore plays hide-and-seek with headlands hiding sheltered coves. Bigbury Bay and Plymouth soon slip by as the rugged isolation of the Cornish cliffs and sandy beaches reach Land's End. Beyond lies the mouth of the English Channel, yawning wide from the French island of Ushant to the Isles of Scilly.

The *Secret Nature of the Channel Shore* sets out to explore the wildlife that inhabits its depths and survives along its wave-splashed margins. Here the Gulf Stream allows subtropical plants and animals to thrive. Lonely rocks, bare in winter, become nurseries throbbing to the calls of summer breeding birds or the plaintive moans of seal pups. The nature of the English Channel is an extraordinary mix of the bizarre and beautiful – seabird cities and shipwrecks, colourful cliffs and seas of sand – all set against a backdrop of spectacular scenery that rivals many a more exotic seaboard.

Some three years' research and field work has gone into the making of this book which accompanies the BBC television series. The result, while it cannot be a definitive natural history of the English Channel, is still a detailed look at some of its more exceptional parts. There is, inevitably, much that it was not possible to capture on film. It is these instances that remain just vivid memories; for instance there were the days I spent alone, stranded on an island in a seething storm with 300 puffins for company and the occasion when I swam with seals. Another time was spent on a remote island in the middle of the night, surrounded by flapping wings and weird choking calls. Even for me, these are not everyday events but a privileged glimpse into another world that thrives around our shores; a world that I share with you in this book.

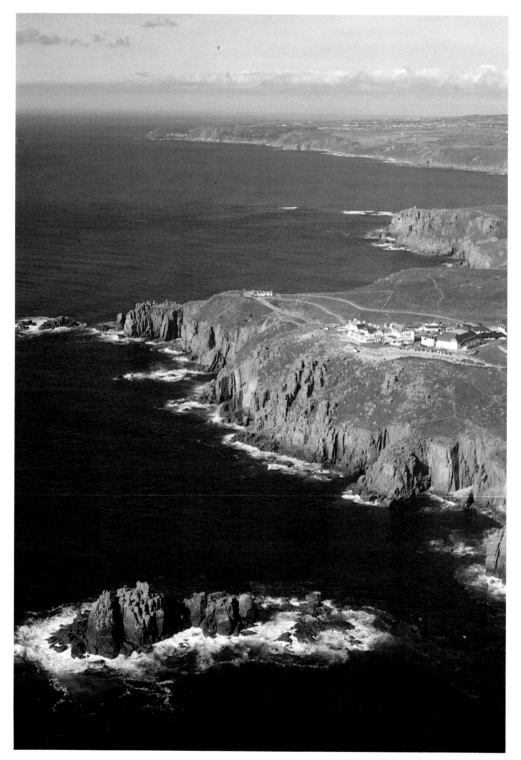

Land's End, Cornwall, the furthest south-westerly point of Britain. The great granite cliffs, exposed to the full force of the Atlantic Ocean, form the leading north-west edge of the English Channel.

CHAPTER ONE

Beyond Tide's Reach

*I*N THE FAR south-west of Britain, beyond the sheer granite cliffs at Land's End, lies the vast expanse of the Atlantic Ocean, bathing Britain in its relentless eastward drift and warm prevailing winds. The currents from the Atlantic owe their origin mainly to the mighty Gulf Stream, which begins in the Caribbean Sea. This shallow water, warmed by a tropical sun, is confined by the eastern coast of Central America and the islands of the West Indies. The rotation of the earth and the unfailing trade winds combine to push the water north and west up past the Yucatán peninsula. Driven by the force of water building up in the Gulf of Mexico, it pours through the narrow straits of Florida at some three and a half knots. A boundless warm river, some 80 kilometres wide and 500 metres deep, the Gulf Stream passes into the colder waters of the western Atlantic. There it spreads into four main currents and gradually loses momentum. After some 7000 kilometres, the Gulf Stream (known strictly as the North Atlantic Drift by this point) reaches the British Isles. The main flow passes up the west coast towards Scotland while another current enters the mouth of the English Channel.

The Gulf Stream helps give rise to the incredible fertility of European seas. Just as on land there are regions of luxuriant green growth, teeming with animal life, and places almost barren, so too there are ocean extremes. The deep Sargasso Sea to the north-east of the Caribbean is one of its deserts, while the coastal waters of Britain are among its lush jungles. This is because the Gulf Stream contributes to upwellings that bring essential nutrients to the surface.

All plants require nitrogen and phosphorus and these nutrients are spread throughout the sea. By far the greatest quantities are held in perpetual darkness at great depths. But plants can only live in the sunlit surface waters because they use sunlight to make their food in a process called photosynthesis. If you dive, even in virtually clear water, light will gradually be lost as you descend. The reds will go first, followed by the oranges and yellows, and at around 25 metres, the greens will disappear as well. Suspended in the eerie gloom of mid-water, you will see above the light surface and below only the blue and black of the abyss. The temperature also drops as you descend through the warm surface water to the cold dark lower layer, extending down to the ocean floor. Between these two distinct zones is a narrow middle layer called the thermocline, in which the temperature drops more sharply. This prevents mixing of the waters above and below, locking away from the plants the nutrients held in the depths. In the clear, calm deep desert of the Sargasso Sea, this barrier is always present. In the coastal waters of Britain, though, a number of factors may combine to break down the thermocline.

Some 300 kilometres south-west of Land's End, the bed of the Atlantic Ocean meets the European continental shelf. The steep rise churns the water, and further turbulence occurs as the warm Gulf Stream passes into the colder coastal waters. Especially in winter, there are storms which agitate the sea still further, bringing cold upwellings from the deep to disrupt the eastward flow of the Gulf Stream into the Channel. Swirls and eddies from top to bottom mix the waters, bringing nutrients to the surface. In these salt waters, life blooms today just as it first did some 3500 million years ago.

We know from fossils that among the first creatures on earth were simple single-celled algae. They can still be found in the seas today, ranging in size from less than 0.2 of a millimetre to a little more than 1 millimetre. They are encased in delicate, intricately formed shells, some built of calcium and others of translucent silica, in an exquisite variety of shapes. These tiny algae, known as phytoplankton, are unable to propel themselves and so simply drift with the currents. The wandering plants contain chlorophyll, which allows them to harness the energy of sunlight to make food and build their tiny bodies. They also need nutrients and, in the Channel, a nourishing ooze is constantly swept up to the algal blooms.

Floating among this marine vegetable soup are vast numbers of equally small animals – the zooplankton. Many are also single-celled, and differ from the algae principally in lacking chlorophyll. They cannot, therefore, make their own food and so eat the algae that do, and each other. More complex zooplankton include tiny worms, small shrimps and miniature jellyfish. Other animals join the floating throng for just one stage of their lives, such as the larvae of barnacles, crabs, worms, starfish and molluscs. All are dispersed by the tide and as the season progresses, they can occur in enormous numbers. A child's bucket holding a litre of sea water could contain several million bacteria, thousands of phytoplankton and hundreds of zooplankton. The entire community is known simply as plankton.

They are some of the smallest life on this planet yet they can profoundly affect our world. To the west of the Channel, vast algal blooms are being monitored from space because it is thought that these tiny organisms can influence our climate. They absorb and scatter the sunlight, warming the upper layers of the sea. The oxygen they produce worldwide is greater than all the vegetation on land. Even more incredible is their production of volatile organic compounds, which are released into the air, helping to form clouds. Their most significant contribution, though, is locking carbon in the oceans on a scale large enough to affect the level of carbon dioxide in the atmosphere. A high level leads to global warming, while a low level allows more of the sun's heat to escape, cooling the planet. The algae's role in the carbon cycle may have helped push the planet into ice ages in the past and could control how fast our climate changes in the future.

Phytoplankton are also vital in another way to marine creatures, because they are at the base of the sea's food web. All sea animals ultimately rely on phytoplankton, although only some exploit directly this rich food source. In shallow water, plankton feeders can remain fixed to the seabed, relying on the movement of tides and currents to bring their food within reach. Barnacles snatch with their feathery arms, mussels and sea squirts suck in and filter it, while sea anemone tentacles gently wave and grope their meal from the soup.

In the open sea where plankton float far above the bottom, those that feed upon them must actively swim, such as small fish. Many fish also become part of the temporary plankton in the earlier stages of their lives. They lay eggs which float to the surface, or whose larvae do so shortly after hatching.

The plankton-eating herring and closely related sprat are northern species of fish and reach their southern limit in the Channel. The pilchard, however, is a warm-water fish and reaches its northern limit in the western approaches to the Channel. These plankton feeders spawn off the south coast of Cornwall, laying floating eggs like the herring and sprat. After hatching, the larval fish at first depend on the food reserves of their yolk sac, drifting with the currents before beginning to actively feed. The range of the pilchard in the English Channel varies with the warmth of the water, a fact which has caused the fortunes of the Cornish pilchard fishing industry to rise and fall three times so far in the twentieth century.

A commercially sought fish that has provided a more dependable harvest is the mackerel, a member of the tunny family. Its aerofoil-like finlets, with depressions into which the crescent-shaped fins fold flat, and the jelly-like surrounds to the eyes, all reduce drag. A sleek body and smooth features are

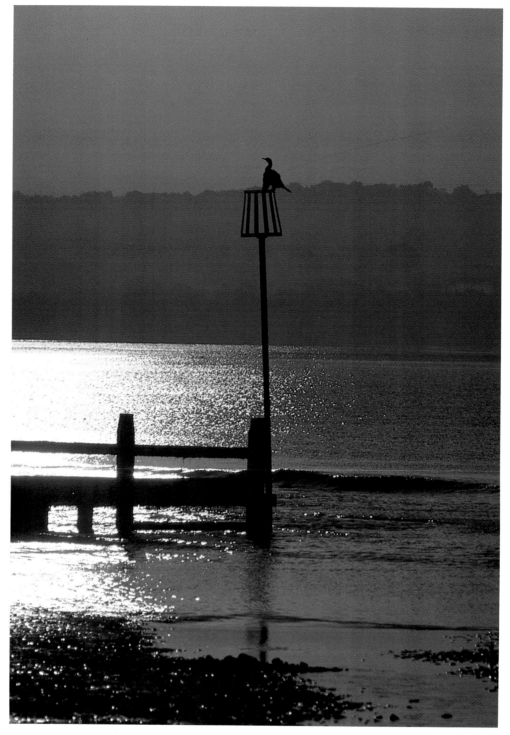

Sunrise at Dawlish Warren in South Devon. A cormorant dries its waterlogged wings after diving for an early morning meal of fish.

built for sustained speed with minimum effort. Mackerel inhabit open water where their silver underside and the iridescent blue-green stripes over their back help to camouflage them from predators. They spawn mainly to the west of the Channel towards the edge of the continental shelf. After breeding they move into coastal waters where they feed voraciously on zooplankton and chase shoals of smaller fish.

Among the mackerel's shallow-water prey is the lesser sand eel, the most common of the five species of sand eel found around the North Atlantic coasts. The sand eels belong to a different group of fish from the true eels, their name coming from their slender shape, which is suited to burrowing. The lesser sand eel spends most of the day in the sand, emerging mainly at night to feed on marine worms and plankton. During summer small shoals of these shiny-scaled little fish can sometimes be seen in the shallows off sandy beaches. At other times their presence is given away by their predators, for like the other small shoaling fish they play an important part in the food chain between plankton and larger marine animals.

Sand eels occur in incalculable numbers and lure many other animals close into the shore. Each year, fishermen trawl hundreds of thousands of tonnes of both lesser and greater sand eels around Britain. These fish are consumed with equal efficiency by plunge-diving terns and paddling kittiwakes, and chased underwater by guillemots, puffins and larger fish. The larger fish then fall prey to other fishermen, are bombarded by wave-piercing gannets, hunted by grey Atlantic seals and, most spectacularly of all, pursued by leaping and diving schools of common dolphin.

Like us, seals and dolphins lie at the end of a food chain. As marine animals get bigger, their prey tends to increase in size, a process that culminates in the top predators. But some large creatures cut out the middle courses and tap the primary source of food in the sea, plankton. One such creature travels so slowly, reaching a top speed of about 5 kilometres an hour, that when people first encountered its floppy-finned lazy pace during the hottest days of summer, they assumed it to be basking in the sun. During warm, calm days in the Channel, the basking shark is one of the most commonly encountered members of its family. For them speed is not important, indeed it is counterproductive, because there is a limit to the rate that plankton can be sieved from the water. An animal travelling too fast will build up a pressure ridge in front, sweeping large numbers of plankton to the side. All that is needed for a nourishing meal is to pass through the fertile broth at a leisurely pace with mouth wide open. The basking shark's huge jaws gape to reveal five gill slits either side of the head.

Swimming just beneath the surface, it takes in up to 1000 tonnes of water an hour which passes through the gills rakers, where slender, horny comb-like bristles filter plankton, and then goes out of the slits. Although individual plankton may be small, the food value in such quantity is huge, as can be judged from the enormous size of this feeder. Basking sharks can grow to a length of 12 metres and a weight of 4 tonnes, making them the second largest fish living today. Only the closely related plankton feeder, the whale shark, grows bigger, up to 20 metres in length.

Basking sharks are formidable-looking creatures, especially when confronted underwater, but these plankton eaters are harmless to humans. Most sharks, though, are sleek, fast-moving predators, ranking among the most savage and efficient marine hunters. They tend to inhabit warm waters and so pose no threat to bathers in Britain's cool waters. Even where they are common, their danger to humans is grossly overrated, although they may accidentally run into a person because sharks have no means of braking. Being unable to stop quickly or to float effortlessly in midwater, they must grab a bite with razor-sharp teeth while swimming at speed.

The most numerous shark of European seas is also one of the smallest. Seldom exceeding 70 centimetres in length and 2 kilograms in weight, the common or lesser spotted dogfish is abundant in the English Channel. Unlike the larger open-water dogfish, it lives close to the seabed, feeding on fish, shellfish and crustaceans. The male spotted dogfish is the same size as the female and during mating, he coils tightly around her. Afterwards, she moves into shallow water and lays her eggs individually while swimming amongst the swaying forests of seaweeds. Each precious embryo is contained within an opaque, rectangular capsule, and held fast to the weed by curled tendrils emanating from the capsule's four corners. The egg case is more commonly known as a mermaid's purse. The eggs hatch five to eleven months later, depending on the temperature of the water.

When a storm brews in the Channel, waves rear their foaming crests and hurl headlong towards the shore, there unleashing energy built up over a thousand miles or more. The sea surges into tiny cracks and crevices, fracturing and exploding the rock face under huge hydraulic pressure. The softer rocks are eroded more quickly than the rest, cutting deep clefts and boring out caves and tunnels in the cliffs. Over the millennia, the land has slowly retreated before the onslaught, leaving hard rock stacks and giant slabs isolated from the mainland. During a storm, exposed cliffs are also subjected to a bombardment of boulders and sand, further exploiting their natural faults and weaknesses.

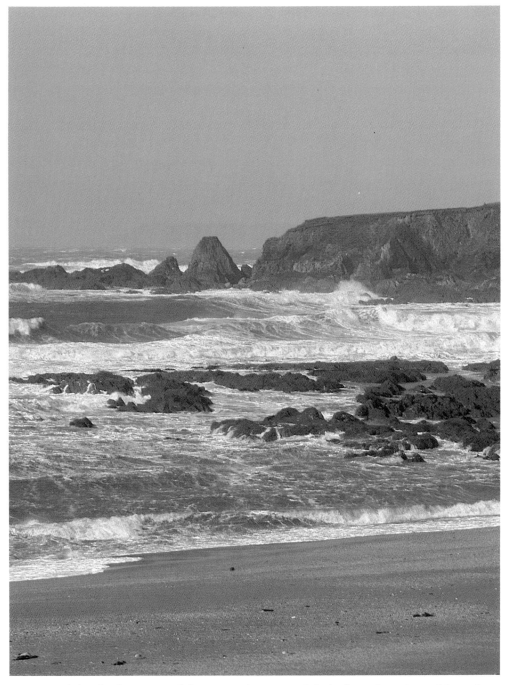

Storms speed the relentless erosion of the coast at the expense of the land. Harder rocks are left standing while softer material gives way; cliffs are shattered and boulders are ground into sand.

The biggest boulders strike at the cliff base, undermining the face until the overhanging rocks finally collapse. For a while they may lie in a protective heap, forming a natural breakwater, but subsequent storms slowly crush and grind them into smaller stones and eventually to sand. This is picked up and transported along the coast by tidal currents, leaving the cliff exposed once more to the unremitting assault of the Atlantic.

Currents and wind-blown waves are the principal forces that have fashioned the character of the coast since the birth of the Channel, some 6000 years ago. The ever changing pattern of the shore is also affected by the structure of headlands and bays, islands and reefs, and by the state of the tide. Most places in Britain have two high-water and two low-water tides every twenty-four hours. These tides are produced by the powerful gravitational pull of the moon, and to a lesser extent of the more distant sun. The world's oceans are attracted towards the moon, resulting in a piling up of the seas on the side closest to this massive satellite and on the earth's opposite side, where the influence of the moon is at its least. At the same time the sea is drawn away from the other parts of the world, and coasts there experience low tide. The daily rhythm of the tides is produced by the orbit of the moon around the earth, and the earth's own daily rotation and annual journey around the sun. While the world rotates every twenty-four hours, it takes a further fifty minutes for the earth and moon to return to approximately the same relative position. So the tidal bulges circumnavigate the world at a progressively later time each day. As a result, the actual time of high or low water at any point depends on the day, the month and the year.

The range of the tide also varies from day to day. The highest are spring tides, a name that derives from the old English word *springan* meaning 'to rise'. They are not confined to the season of spring, but occur twice a month throughout the year, whenever there is a full or new moon. At this time, the sun and moon are roughly in line and their gravitational pulls are combined. In between, when the sun and moon are at right angles to the earth, the forces of these celestial bodies work against each other to produce neap tides, which have the lowest tidal range.

The average range of spring tides around the shores of most of Britain is around 2–3 metres, but there is much variation. While the south-west coast of Scotland has a tidal range of barely 1.5 metres, much of the south coast of England experiences a range of over 5 metres. The funnelling effect of the Channel can increase that to some 7 metres at Folkestone. Even that is small compared with tidal ranges on the other side of the Channel, which can be among the greatest in the world. The edge of the harbour wall in St Helier, Jersey, is no place to be if you suffer from a fear of heights, because an ebbing spring tide can lower the water over 12 metres, leaving you perched on a structure some four storeys above the sea.

The ebb and flow of tides has the most profound effect on the margin of the land. Twice daily a vast region of the seabed is exposed to the air, and twice it is drowned. Animals and plants that live in this littoral or intertidal zone, bounded by high and low water marks, are well suited to such extremes. They have to be, to survive in one of the harshest environments in the world. The marine life higher up the shore endures greater stress, spending a longer time parched by a hot sun and drying wind, and washed in the saltless water of rain. Further down the shore the time exposed to the air gradually reduces, producing a series of distinct zones. Each is inhabited by plants and animals best able to exploit that particular band, the most obvious usually being marine algae.

At low tide, swathes of marine algae hang limp, clothing the rocks in a slippery carpet of plants that are called, almost disparagingly, seaweeds. When the tide floods, they are transformed, their drab fronds lifting once more to sway with the movement of the waves and blow about in the currents. Their watery environment differs dramatically from that of their land-living relatives, and so too do the plants themselves. On land, most of a plant's tissue growth goes into supporting its structure, and collecting and distributing precious water. But in the sea roots, stems, leaves and flamboyant flowers are superfluous. Surrounded and supported by water, marine algae have no lack of liquid. The sea also provides a means of cross-fertilisation and dispersal when the plants propagate. Seaweeds do require light, and so many either float or attach themselves to the bottom or to each other in relatively shallow water.

There are about 700 different types of marine algae around the coast of Britain. Plants are the principal source of food for animals and, on land, an area so lush with growth would be heavily grazed. In contrast, seaweeds allow some marine animals to survive between the tides but they are far from fully exploited. This is because phytoplankton form the basis of the food chain at sea. As a result, many seaweeds survive only to be torn apart by the sea and their tattered fragments may eventually enrich the seabed for bottom-dwelling worms and crustaceans. Bigger bits of weed may float for weeks, providing temporary shade and shelter for small fish. The rest, along with an assortment of natural and manmade flotsam and jetsam, is cast up somewhere on a shore.

Most beaches have a strandline – a ribbon of weed and marine litter left high and drying after the tide has turned. There are certain shores where all life seems at times to be stranded. Especially after a storm, great piles of marine debris are thrown up by the waves and then abandoned by the sea. In the autumn kelps shed their fronds, and at other times of the year whole plants complete with holdfasts and heaps of wracks are ripped from coastal rocks. Mixed with red and green seaweeds all slowly bleach in the sun while rotting away.

Some shores are well known as shell beaches, where waves and tides combine to throw up massive quantities of empty mollusc homes. Clusters of egg capsules laid by molluscs, and a colourful collection of their intricately sculpted shells, appear at times to be sorted and carefully strewn along the tideline. It is also wave action and currents that deposit objects of similar size and weight close to each other. In time they are smashed and fragmented by the surge and backwash of the surf, the broken bits being ground smaller and smaller before they finally merge with the sand.

Each high tide brings a new supply of seaweed to replenish the strandline, by the tonne in rough weather or just a few fronds when becalmed. After several days of constant wind from the west, the tide can leave evidence of the Gulf Stream's distant and exotic origin. Many tropical rivers are fringed with trees that depend largely on fast-flowing water to disperse their seeds. Such seeds must be tough, able to withstand long periods of immersion, until washed ashore on suitable mud where they can eventually take root and grow. Some are carried too far, such as big *Macuna* and *Entada* beans from the Caribbean and Central America, which are not uncommon finds on Channel shores.

Wind is used as a means of propulsion by some warm-water marine organisms and they too can be pushed too far, ending up as beached gelatinous blobs that bear little resemblance to once free-floating animals. The violet sea snail floats beneath a mucous-blown raft of bubbles in search of its favoured prey, by-the-wind sailors. These appropriately named creatures have an oval membraneous float from beneath which hang short tentacles and a central mouth. The float supports a stiff little triangular sail which catches the wind. The translucent blue by-the-wind sailors appear at first glance to be small jellyfish, but belong to an entirely different group, known as the siphonophores. They are complex colonial animals made up of many individuals, or polyps, each modified to carry out a particular function. Some are for attack, others for feeding, reproduction, suspension or movement. Unlike true jellyfish, they cannot swim and so just drift with the ocean breeze. They are closely related to the larger and more

*On Tresco in the Isles of Scilly (*opposite*), as on almost every beach, the receding tide leaves a strandline of washed-up seaweed and marine debris, a beachcomber's delight.*

deadly *Physalia* or Portuguese man-of-war. This has a gas-filled bag and purplish crest, which act as sail and float for a tangling trail of stinging tentacles that in some cases reach an incredible 60 metres in length. In contrast to the benign by-the-wind sailors, an encounter with the almost transparent *Physalia* tentacles can be agonising for people.

Portuguese man-of-war are relished, though, by large leathery turtles. Since records began in the south-west of England back in 1756, turtles have been regularly sighted around the coast. Of the five species infrequently found in British waters – the common loggerhead, Kemp's ridley, green, hawkesbill and leathery turtles – the last is most commonly seen. The leathery turtle is so-called because its carapace is covered with a tough leathery skin, unlike the bony shell with embedded polygonal plates possessed by other turtles.

Mainly confined to warm waters, marine turtles are descended from land-dwelling, air-breathing tortoises. Over millions of years they have become superbly adapted sea-going creatures. But, like all reptiles, they must still come on land to breed because if submerged, their embryos would suffocate and die. The eggs can only develop and hatch where gaseous oxygen can pass through the shell, enabling the embryo to breathe. So each year, across the oceans of the world, female turtles return to the beach of their own birth to lay their eggs in the sand. The few favoured breeding locations, known as rookeries, are used by generation after generation of turtles.

The rookeries of leathery turtles are few and far between. The main Atlantic site is on the South American coast of French Guiana, where 6000 regularly breed. There are other smaller sites, scattered across the Caribbean and even in the Mediterranean. So leathery turtles must regularly encounter the Gulf Stream. They are powerful swimmers, using long, broad flippers to propel themselves at great speed underwater. They are also capable of diving to immense depths, having been recorded at 1200 metres, where water temperatures globally are below 5°C. To do this, they must be able to hold their breath for at least one hour and withstand cold water.

Many leathery turtles have been injured or caught in fishing nets off the Cornish coast, where average sea surface temperatures in winter are around 9°C. While they are highly unlikely to come there to breed they undoubtedly hunt the depths for their favourite food, jellyfish. Catches of jellyfish in trawl nets from between 800 and 1500 metres indicate that vast numbers are present in deep water. It has been suggested that jellyfish and other similar species, capable of luminescence, produce enough light for the nomadic turtles to home in on the glow of their prey in the darkness of the abyss.

Leathery turtles are found on British beaches but most are dead on arrival. The relative scarcity of jellyfish in shallow water perhaps accounts for the empty stomachs of these sad strandings. In certain years, however, swarms of jellyfish, carried by the Gulf Stream, arrive in huge numbers off Channel coasts. Warm dry summers in particular are noted jellyfish and turtle years, 1988 bringing almost an invasion with sixteen confirmed sightings of adult leathery turtles in Cornwall alone.

The remains of dead turtles, fish, mollusc eggs, crabs and other crustaceans provide a supply of rich pickings that varies with each season and each tide. For the majority of marine creatures the strandline is beyond reach, but there are some animals that scavenge the shore, such as sandhoppers. If you disturb a piece of weed along the strandline by day, a hopping horde of these aptly named amphipods will leap into action. Relatives of shrimps, sandhoppers appear to be curled up and sideways compressed, a shape which probably helps them to burrow in sand. The power for their exuberant jumps, at times over 2 metres, is provided by just three stiff pairs of their many appendages. They breed between May and August, and the females can produce up to four broods of seventeen young each year, which are retained in her special brood pouch. Until the young are large enough to fend for themselves, the females remain in their burrows. Sandhoppers obtain all the moisture their bodies require from damp sand. They hide in it from the heat of the sun by day, often beneath wave-heaped piles of seaweed, and emerge after dark. In the cool air of night, sandhoppers swarm in numbers up to 25 000 on each square metre of sand, feasting on decaying weed and rotting flesh.

Kelp flies can occur in equally large numbers. Thousands of these insects sometimes migrate over short distances along the shore, perhaps when an exceptionally high tide soaks their strandline home. They are usually found flying close to the sand, buzzing around stranded weed. Seven different species of kelp flies have been identified living exclusively around beaches. They lay their eggs in rotting seaweed for the larvae to consume the fronds, so hastening the weeds' eventual decay.

Neither sandhoppers nor kelp flies pose any real threat to people lounging about on the beach, and are only a nuisance to those who sit too close to the strandline. It has been found, however, that kelp flies can be attracted by certain aromatic smells during the day, and sandhoppers to light at night. Dry driftwood is regularly collected for fires. Barbecues glowing brightly down on the shore, seem particularly inviting to nocturnal, hopping beach-dwellers. As some sandhoppers can also bite, they can really get the party going – elsewhere.

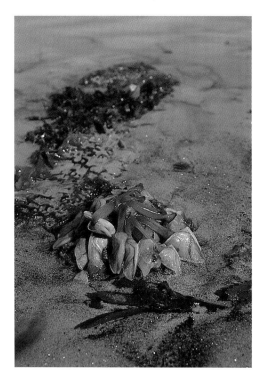

Left: *Goose barnacles attached to a piece of floating wood have drifted from the warmer parts of the Atlantic.*

Below: *Stranded shell of a violet sea snail and the remains of a 'by-the-wind sailor' on which they feed.*

Right: *Groynes slow the shifting of sand by strong currents and so help to retain the beach.*

Driftwood arrives on the beach in all shapes and sizes. There are planks washed from harbours and decks, shipwrecks and pieces of pier, and even entire trees, torn from a river bank by a raging flood. The most collectable of all are the fantastically twisted weather-worn branches and roots. Some bits of wood may have drifted for weeks, months or even years, voyaging thousands of miles and perhaps being stranded on remote exotic shores before being reclaimed, once again, by the sea. Such wood becomes a floating home for many marine organisms. One of the most notorious for the damage it can cause to unprotected wooden boats and piers is the shipworm, *Teredo*. This creature has been known and loathed since classical times, when it riddled the planking of Greek triremes and Roman galleys. Much later the shipworm succeeded where the Spanish Armada failed: Sir Francis Drake's ship, *The Golden Hind*, was eaten away under his feet.

Despite their name, they are not worms but bivalve molluscs. In the tropics some species can grow up to an incredible 1.5 metres in length. Thankfully for British boatmen, only three species are found in European waters, and the biggest of these grow only up to 20 centimetres. All start life as part of the plankton until chance brings them in contact with timber. When fully grown, they can bore a finger-sized hole through solid wood, from an easily overlooked little entrance.

Some driftwood passengers do not damage their raft, but simply hang on for the ride. These include the acorn or goose barnacles, which come from the warmer parts of the Atlantic. These elegant creatures bear a curious resemblance to a bird's head and neck, and were thought in the past to be juvenile forms of barnacle geese. Hence the geese were regarded as fish, a belief that no doubt continued long beyond the revelation of the truth, because it meant that barnacle geese could be eaten on Fridays and feast days with a clear Catholic conscience. At one time goose barnacles attached themselves, sometimes in huge numbers, to the bottoms of slow-moving sailing ships, impeding their performance and adding substantially to the duration of a voyage. Today they are more likely to be found clinging to a small piece of wood or maybe a bottle. Like more conventional barnacles, they feed by opening their plates and extending feathery appendages known as cirri to grasp at floating plankton.

The strandline is the final resting place for many driftwood passengers and other marine plants and animals. Apart from the multitude of smaller creatures that end their lives on a remote shore, large mammals may also be beached. Dead and dying seals, whales and dolphins are all at times left by the tide. Most of these perish from natural causes, such as old age and disease, while some are the victims of accidents, such as collisions with boats or, increasingly, becoming entangled in fishing nets. Rarer and perhaps much more distressing are the groups of healthy whales, dolphins and porpoises that end their days on land. Of the 3000 incidents of strandings reported in the UK over the last seventy years, only 137 have been of live animals, and of those only twenty-eight involved a group of three or more.

The reasons for the apparently intentional mass strandings by sea-going mammals are difficult to fathom. We know that dolphins, in particular, use echo-location to detect their prey and that this technique also makes them extraordinarily aware of their surroundings. However, it has been suggested that whales and dolphins navigate to some extent using natural variations in the earth's magnetic field. They do not simply use it as a compass to detect north, but can read it like a map, sensing subtle differences in magnetic strengths and following magnetic contours underwater. Since most major strandings seem to occur where the earth's magnetic field lines run parallel to the coast, it is probable that they are, in fact, accidents of map reading.

Boxes and crates, bottles, cans and fishing nets are also regularly washed ashore. The amount of maritime litter on the strandline is increasing and, as in the past, it is a valuable source of material for people living on the coast. Nature too has its shore scavengers, including turnstones. These birds are named for their habit of flipping over pebbles and weed in the frantic search for insects and tiny crustaceans. If it is too heavy for the beak, a larger stone may be moved by pushing with the breast. They will prise open shells and even extract flesh from carcasses. Turnstones are one of the most distinctive birds of the shore and are noted long-distance travellers. Their nesting range spans the arctic from Alaska, eastward to Siberia. After breeding they migrate south, spending the winter months on the coasts of the western Atlantic and are to be found turning weeds and stones on warm-water shores around the world.

In Britain, turnstones are often joined on the strandline by flocks of starlings and foraging rock pipits. During winter the rotting heaps of weed generate warmth, which allows many insects to survive the cold weather and these in turn provide food for hungry birds. In midsummer, swallows can be seen skimming just above the sand, following the strandline to catch mouthfuls of kelp flies. By night rats scurry down after the tide to scavenge the sea's offerings. On some coasts even hedgehogs may amble along the shore. Foxes are far more frequently seen, checking the strandline as part of their nocturnal routine.

In isolated coves and on sands seldom trodden by people in Devon and

Cornwall, the footprints of one of England's most elusive and sadly rare mammals can be found – the otter. Although almost completely nocturnal in England and mainly confined to freshwater, they occur regularly during daylight hours in Scotland and Ireland on quiet stretches of coast. Otters are known to give birth to their young in sea caves in Cornwall, and can occasionally be seen from the cliff tops, gambolling down on the shore. Too far away to hear the intrusive sound of human voices or catch our scent, a pair of otters were watched playing for nearly an hour on a beach at the foot of steep cliffs. They raced and chased each other along the beach and boulder-strewn shore, pushing and wriggling amongst piles of kelp, until the sound of a distant barking dog caused them to vanish as suddenly as they had appeared. Such sightings along Channel shores are rare, but rock pools and the strandlines left at low tide must at times be tempting larders for otters. Apart from fish which make up a large part of their diet, shore crabs also feature on their menu.

Most animals visit the strandline only after dark and in the early morning, mainly due to the presence of a creature that migrates each summer in increasing numbers to the seaside. People flock to popular holiday destinations all along the sunny south coast of Britain at predictable times of the year. Some animals take advantage of this seasonal surge in edible litter, regularly raiding bins and searching the shore for carelessly strewn pieces of picnics. After the last flasks of tea have been drained, and deckchairs, windbreaks and towels folded, the gulls move in. Raucous herring and common gulls, and even lesser and some greater blackbacks, scavenge greedily for the best leftovers. Once the sun has set the nightshift arrives, including the foxes which seem to have developed an insatiable appetite for spicy fried chicken and chips.

On less busy beaches, small birds can continue their feeding all day. If disturbed, they will simply move further along the strandline. However, to breed in such a precariously open space requires a shore that is unlikely to be visited by holiday makers and a nest that is all but invisible. The ringed plover uses no nest material at all, laying its cryptically coloured eggs in a shallow scrape on the bare sand or shingle. As you walk along a shore often the first indication of a nest site will be an adult plover fluttering ahead, looking injured. With this broken-wing display, the bird cleverly leads you away from its nest. When you have passed far enough away to no longer threaten its eggs or young, the ringed plover will suddenly cease its avian theatrics and fly. Regular disturbance seems to be the main reason for the decline of the beach breeding success of these attractive little birds.

The strandline is such a familiar feature of the coastline that it is easily

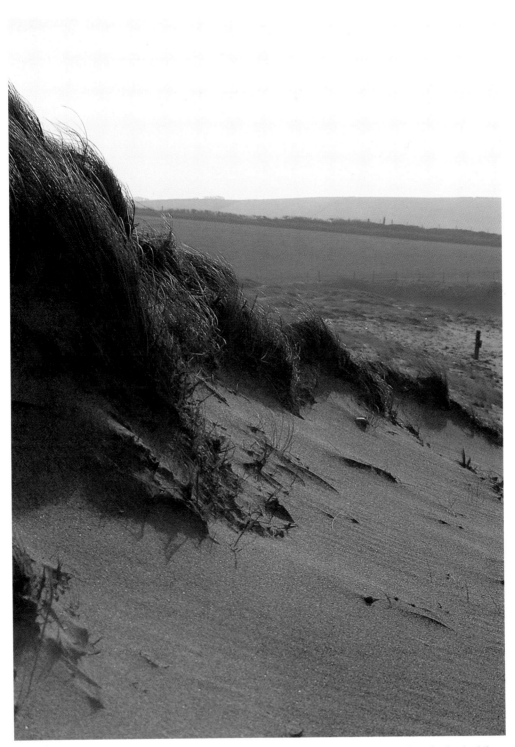

The wind is both a builder and destroyer of the dunes. Gales sweep vast quantities of sand inland while the sea breeze brings a more constant supply, and where marram grass slows the movement to a trickle, dunes grow. Once established, other plants take root and bind the sands still further.

overlooked, but it cannot be ignored by one of the senses. That healthy bracing smell of the seaside, blowing up the beach from the surf, is not so much the scent of sun, sand and waves, as the stench of rotting seaweed. However, as far as most people are concerned, sand is the essential ingredient for a good beach. If you pick up a handful, the mixture of finely ground grains of rock and fragments of shells that runs through your fingers has a quality quite different from that of other beaches nearby. Although it is all carried by currents, deposited by waves and blown by the wind, sand has a character and composition unique to each shore.

For creatures on the seabed, the effect of the motion of waves at the surface increases the shallower they go. Even in summer calms, every passing wave and each tide ceaselessly stirs the surface particles of inshore sand, preventing seaweeds from settling and sedentary animals, such as barnacles, sponges and sea squirts, from gaining a grip. Crabs and other creatures that lurk in the shelter of rock pools venture out on to the sandy expanses at their peril. So fine sandy beaches, laid bare by the falling tide, look barren and devoid of life. Even to a swimmer with mask and flippers, gliding above rippled sand in the clear shallow water of an incoming tide, the bed will appear at first glance as empty as a desert. However, like its arid counterpart, it does contain life. Segmented worms, shrimps, shellfish and urchins make up the majority of sand-dwellers, but they often escape detection because most are burrowers. Safe inside the sand, they are protected from pounding waves and predatory fish, and from drying out at low tide.

The movement of sand by waves and currents in the sea is continued onshore by the breeze. Fine grains swept by gusts and eddies gradually gather into great piles. These may reach over 30 metres in height, yet winds can move entire dunes. Sand blown up the gentle windward slope pours over the crest. Then, in a series of miniature landslips, the dry torrent slides down the steep face and the dune edges slowly forward. Battered and blasted by high winds, with new supplies of sand being thrown ashore by the sea, lines of dunes advance inland.

Legends tell of a series of storms that swept the English Channel for several days causing vast areas of low-lying land to be overwhelmed by huge waves of wind-blown sand. The truth is probably not quite so dramatic or sudden, but equally devastating. Ever since the formation of the Channel, the prevailing winds have blown sand inshore. Reinforcing ancient records, evidence does show that inundation by sand has been greater in some centuries than in others. In the last few hundred years buildings are known to have been buried by advancing sand dunes. They are unlikely to be the last and were certainly not the first. In St Ouen, on the island of Jersey 5000 years ago, prehistoric people abandoned their settlements to the encroaching sand. Menhirs and piles of pottery have been discovered drowned in the dunes. And down on the present-day shore, after rough seas have scoured the beach away, the stumps and roots of an ancient forest can still be seen. Remains of that coastal woodland, destroyed by rising sea levels in the centuries following the last ice age, can also be found from time to time across the Channel. At Thurlestone on the shores of Devon, a severe winter gale exposed a great tract of peat and twisted tree roots for just a few short weeks before it was buried again.

When sand is on the move it seems as if nothing on earth will stop it. But plants can, or at least they can slow the movement to a trickle, by trapping and binding the particles. Consolidation begins down on the shore, where the decomposing strandline produces a drain of rich nutrients that leach into the sun-parched sand. Only a few plants can survive the hostile and extreme conditions between land and sea. There is no soil or humus, and little mineral content in sand except for the remains of shells. Clear cloudless skies permit the sun to bake the beach, so that at midday the surface temperature of sand can exceed 60°C, while at night it can plummet. Desiccating winds blow unabated from the sea and the dry, salty sand is constantly shifting. Only during summer months, when this area is beyond the tide's reach, can a few plant species take root. Sea rocket and saltwort rise from bare grains along with orache and the creeping sea-convolvulus. Sea spurge and the rarer sea stock are both found at the top of the shore, while the leathery-leaved sea holly, with its striking blue flower, produces seeds which are dispersed by the tide.

One of the most important of the foreshore pioneers is the sea couch grass, which has an ability to grow with the foundation of a dune. Spreading by means of horizontal rhizomes that send up shoots, it steadily traps sand between its leaves. For a while the growth of the couch grass keeps pace with the build up of the embryo dune. However, its maximum height is about half a metre and as the dunes begin to grow taller than this, marram grass takes over. Of all the plants that live in sand, marram is the dominant builder of dunes.

Marram grass spreads by extensive systems of rhizomes, from which metre-length leaves grow up. Its adventitious roots collect what moisture they can from between the particles of sand. This plant can survive even in the most severe conditions, where wind-blown sand smothers the growth in a layer that may at times be metres deep. Buds at the base of the leaves produce shoots, which break through to the surface and there grow a new tuft of leaves. The structure of those leaves helps the plant to withstand a danger faced by all desert dwellers

– drought. The thick cuticle helps to reduce water loss. While the stomata – tiny holes through which the plant transpires – are hidden in deep pits surrounded by spines. Hinged cells curl the leaf as the humidity drops, further reducing the loss of precious water. As marram grass spreads, so the erosion of sand by the wind is diminished. This increases the stability of the surface and creates a milder microclimate amongst the marram's jungle of leaves, both of which allow other less tolerant plants to share the colonisation of the so-called yellow dunes.

Few animals can survive the conditions tolerated by the front-line dune-building plants, and still fewer can consume the tough long leaves of marram. But where the shattered remnants of seashells form part of the sand, snails exploit this source of calcium to build their own mobile homes. In the drier dunes garden snails look strangely out of place, while in damper parts, brown-lipped snails occur in a bewildering variety of banded shells. When surface temperatures soar, some snails remain in the cooler air above the ground attached to the stems of marram. Also perched there are the great green bush cricket and grasshoppers, including the common, ground and mottled, all of which can be heard rather than seen. Other animals keep clear of the sandy surface during the heat of the day by digging just a few centimetres deep, where it can be considerably cooler because sand is a poor conductor of heat.

Some sandhill snails bury themselves on hot days, as do several different kinds of solitary wasps that are known to live around sand. One, with quivering antennae and wings, is often seen running actively over the sand. The female of the species is the most deadly. Although harmless to humans, she is lethal to spiders, which she starts hunting after mating early in the summer. She drives her prey from a web or pillages them from burrows. The chase ends when the wasp grabs the spider from behind, curls her abdomen round and stings the victim on its soft underside, paralysing it with poison. She then flies the spider to a suitable site and proceeds to excavate a burrow in the sand. The immobilised spider is dragged down the tunnel and the wasp lays a single egg on its underside. She then reseals the chamber and scatters sand outside, before leaving to repeat the performance several more times. Other sand wasps provision their nest with a regular assortment of larvae and caterpillars.

The ubiquitous rabbit digs the biggest network of burrows in the sand, and also contributes to the scant fertility of the dunes. Along with a rotting tangle of marram grass leaves, rabbit droppings play a vital part in building up the organic content of the dunes. Gulls, nesting or flying overhead, add their messy nitrogen-rich gifts. This gradual formation of a thin crust of soil is the next stage in the sand dunes' slow progression towards fertile land. The marram that has

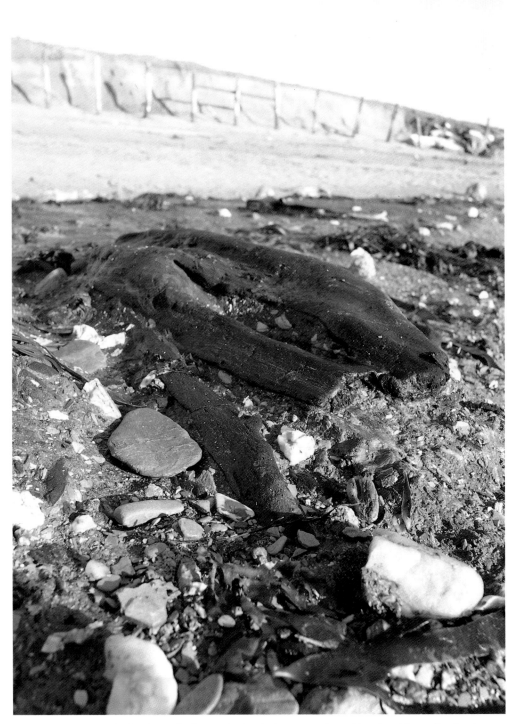

Scoured by a storm, the beach at Thurlestone in South Devon reveals prehistoric evidence of a forest drowned in the final flooding of the English Channel. A bed of peat, twisted roots and fallen trunks lie briefly exposed after several thousands of years preserved in seawater and sand.

helped build the dunes then gives way to other plant species because, ironically, it is dependent on the continual deposition of sand to thrive.

As the sand becomes increasingly sullied, yellow gives way to grey in both colour and name for this particular type of dune. But the shallow and fragile soil can still only support plants tolerant of impoverished conditions. Sand sedges predominate in the decline of the marram, and fescue grass and common cat's ear are widespread. The yellow flowering ragwort adds a bright splash of colour to the grey dunes. Unwelcome on farmland where its poisonous cells are a real danger to cattle, this plant is feasted on with impunity by one creature of the dunes. Having consumed the ragwort's poison, the cinnabar caterpillar can afford to advertise its presence with alternate bands of yellow and black, which warn predators that it is unpalatable. The adult black and red cinnabar moth is no less extravagantly coloured.

Some plants that are unsuited to drought conditions survive on the grey dunes by avoiding the dry summer months. The mouse-ear chickweed, for example, is an annual which flowers in early spring, leaving seeds to germinate in the autumn when rain is more plentiful. Beyond the grey dunes are the sheltered flats of the shore, known as the slacks. Here the soil is thicker and more stable, but still relatively low in nutrients, and the surface, being closer to the water-table, is often flooded in winter. Where the slacks are continually waterlogged, bog-like conditions prevail with mosses, ferns and heathers attracting fox moths and heather beetles. In damper ground orchids also thrive, sending up spectacular stalks of flowers. Trees too may take root, the stands of grey willow and alder providing still more shelter. On better-drained flats, an alkaline soil gives rise to a very different flora, including creeping bent grass, pennyworts, sedges, common daisy and the colourful birdsfoot trefoil, which has brilliant yellow flowers, tinged with red. Creeping willow growing into densely packed bushes may eventually dominate this type of dune slack.

In the lowest parts, where the water-table rises near to the surface, oases form in these English deserts. The permanent and temporary freshwater pools bring new life to the dunes, producing immense numbers of amphibians each year. Frogs are the first to breed almost everywhere, followed closely by common toads and then newts. The rarer natterjack toads are the last to arrive and inhabit just a few special sites. The frogs and toads move to the shore mainly in the cool damp of a rainy night at certain times from early spring to the beginning of summer. Hopping and crawling or, in the case of the natterjacks, running in short bursts, the annual migration ends where the croaking chorus begins – in the dune slack ponds. The wriggling masses of tadpoles, which result from the few frantic days of the amphibians' gathering, scatter in the shallows. At first they feed on the blooming algal growth, but it is a race against time. Summer rainfall on the coast is low or even non-existent for weeks on end and in hot weather, the shallow water evaporates fast. The tadpoles consume as much green algae as they can in the shrinking pools along with the many small crustaceans that live amongst the weed. Like all growing animals, the tadpoles require a good source of protein and will even consume each other. Eventually, escape from a drying pond is made possible for the tadpoles by a remarkable transformation, which provides them with basic features for survival out of water. After growing legs and lungs, and absorbing their tails, they emerge from the dwindling puddles to thrive on a summer feast of small flies.

While underwater, tadpoles are preyed upon by many other creatures, including the adults of other amphibians. The losses are legion, and less than one tadpole in a hundred is likely to take its first gulp of air. Insects are the main bandits in the tadpoles' world. They lurk amongst the growing vegetation, waiting for a wriggling meal to venture close enough to grasp. Waterbeetle larvae and adults dine almost exclusively on tadpoles in some pools, but the most voracious pond-dwelling carnivore is the aquatic nymph of the dragonfly. Stalking the shallow water, cloaked in green slime, its large eyes detect the smallest move. Its mouthparts are unique, and contain a deadly apparatus, an extensible lower lip or mask that can reach out with astonishing speed to snatch and hold its next meal.

Oases occur in the slacks at Dawlish Warren, a sand spit of dunes reaching across the mouth of the Exe estuary in Devon. As the sun sets there in midsummer, a dragonfly nymph, one of perhaps thousands across the country that evening, peers from the pond surface at the gathering gloom. After spending up to two years underwater the time has come for it to emerge. It is a scene little changed since dinosaurs first trod sand.

Dawn brings a warm, drying sun to the glistening dew-drenched wings of the new dragonfly. Looking pale at first, the dragonfly's full colours will develop after a few days. By then, like the other hawker and darter dragonflies, it will be an accomplished flier, able to hover or chase at speed the small insects it takes on the wing. The impressive aerodynamics of dragonflies contrast with the fluttering flight of the closely related damselfly. There are some sixteen different species of these winged dragons and damsels on Dawlish dunes, and their colours are as vivid as some of their names – azure, emerald, red and blue. But they are not the only colourful creatures on the wing.

Of the 2000 or so species of invertebrates found at Dawlish Warren alone, 102

Left: *The little grebe, also known as the dabchick, breeds regularly in the ponds at Dawlish Warren. They build a raft of vegetation for a nest.*

Right: *The distinctive bold coloration of the cinnabar moth caterpillar serves as a warning to birds of their unpleasant taste.*

Left: *A garden escape, the flowers of evening primrose open at dusk and overnight. Early morning catches the blooms before they wither with the rising sun.*

Below: *The sand crocus is the most famous of all the flowers at Dawlish Warren. It is certainly the rarest, as it is found nowhere else on the mainland of Britain.*

different butterflies and moths have been recorded. Some pause only as they pass through to sip nectar from flowers, while others are resident, completing their life cycle among the dunes. Their caterpillars expand as they grow, eating as much as they can in the shortest possible time. Many species of caterpillar are dependent on one type of plant, but a few are not so fussy. One of the less fickle is the hairy caterpillar of the garden tiger moth, which will eat its way through a wide variety of plants. Better known as the woolly bear, this caterpillar hatches from eggs laid in August and hibernates over winter to emerge the following spring. In certain years, large numbers of fully grown woolly bears may be seen crossing the sand, a hairy troop parading in search of a suitable site to pupate.

Although often unpredictable, such mass migrations are not uncommon in the insect world, and some are on a much larger scale. Hot dry summers produce even bigger influxes of continental butterflies than usual. The painted ladies, red admirals and white butterflies that cross the Channel annually are joined once in a while by a host of clouded yellows. While the smoke of war lingered in Europe, the hazy summer heat of 1941 saw one of the greatest influxes of these butterflies along the south coast. Millions turned dunes and parts of the Devon and Cornwall coastline yellow, in the most successful invasion of British shores seen during the Second World War. It was during this time that massive defences were built along Channel beaches to stop human invaders. Barbed wire, metal girders, mines and millions of tonnes of reinforced concrete were cast upon the shores. None were more substantial, or longer lasting, that the walls built along the northern coast of France and in the Channel Islands. Even today these fortifications still effectively cut off vast areas of dunes from the sea. At Dawlish Warren the only reminders of those troubled times are a few lonely pill boxes that were once at the back of an open beach and are now hidden inland.

The last fifty years has seen great changes in the low-lying centre of the warren. It has turned from a muddy tidal inlet to open saltmarsh, then to freshwater wetlands and more recently to grass and scrub. This gradual progression towards dry land is not uniform, for in places the sea is winning and the coast is losing ground. Reinforcements are sometimes deemed necessary to slow the rate of erosion, and today there are walls and groynes built to retain the sand and keep the sea at bay.

Many dunes are designated nature reserves and some have wider uses. Dawlish Warren, for example, contains a golf course as well as a site of special scientific interest. There is a visitors' centre at the warren and wardens to manage and enhance the wildlife, while enlightening the hundreds of holidaymakers and local people who regularly enjoy the dunes. The 450 different types of flowering plants, eight ferns, thirty-six mosses and liverworts and twenty-four species of lichen recorded there so far reflects the diversity of the landscape. Strandline and mobile sand, yellow and grey dunes, slacks, saltmarsh, scrub and freshwater, each has its own distinct nature. Together they create a remarkable richness in a relatively small area. Despite this, the warren's real claim to fame is a flower found nowhere else on mainland Britain. The sand crocus opens its tiny blue flower only in the brightest sun, as befits a plant more at home on the southern coasts of France and Spain. This plant actually seems to benefit from being trodden under foot, for it thrives as much on the shoe-spiked fairways of the golf course as in fenced-off parts of the reserve.

Much of the life, and the dunes themselves, are less resilient, and their greatest threat is the annual invasion of people. Summer brings the liquid song of skylarks and the tramp of human feet marching over the thin protective soil of the dunes. Once the surface soil and underlying mesh of roots are torn, whether by people playing, dogs digging or rabbits nibbling, their grip on the sand is loosened. Then the elements that helped create the dunes attempt to destroy them. A single footprint can be blasted into a huge hole by gale force winds. When such a blow-out is in progress, sand is steadily eroded from the centre and more slumps in from the sides. Eating away at the edge of the breach in the dunes, the drying winds expose more roots to die, releasing yet more sand to be blown away. Eventually, blow-outs can reach 40 metres across, decimating large parts of the dunes.

The value of marram grass in stabilising dunes has been known for centuries. More recently along the coast of the English Channel, as elsewhere in Britain, a programme of replanting and the positioning of duck-board paths and the fencing of vulnerable places, has proved necessary to reduce the erosion. The artificial consolidation of sand is usually an expensive operation, but at Dawlish the annual glut of dead Christmas trees is used to surprisingly good effect. Piled into gaping holes in the dunes, the tangled mesh of branches soon traps the sand, prevents further erosion and hastens the spread of stabilising plants. However, if left to its own devices nature will, in time, effect a cure. The release of sand in a blow-out stimulates the processes of renewal. Marram grass, the dune builder, invades the bare sand and the natural cycle of dune succession begins all over again.

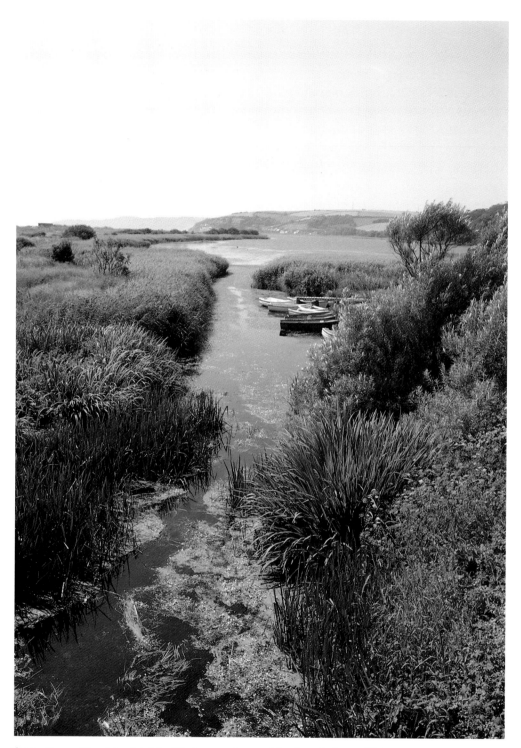

Slapton Ley, a Site of Special Scientific Interest, is owned by the Whitley Wildlife Trust and managed as a nature reserve by the Field Centre. Its importance lies in the rich variety of its nature, from open water, reedbeds and marsh to woodlands and shingle ridge.

CHAPTER TWO

Pure Lagoon

*T*HE PREVAILING WINDS in the Channel blow from the south-west and bring warm moist air from across the Atlantic. This may build into clouds and deliver rain as it rises up over the land. Each raindrop is almost pure water, containing just a little carbon dioxide and oxygen absorbed as it fell through the air. Such freshwater is the lifeblood of the land and its vessels are a merging network of streams and rivers that flow across its surface. Yet freshwater makes up a meagre 3 per cent of all the water on earth, and most is destined to rejoin the other 97 per cent in the salty sea.

When a fresh shower starts, the rain may fall in a fine drizzle and slowly seep into the ground. There it picks up minerals and organic matter dissolved or carried in suspension, eventually acquiring enough nutrients to support and sustain life. As the shower continues the rain may build into a deluge. Then the ground becomes waterlogged and, instead of soaking into the soil, the rain runs across its surface. Trickles quickly become torrents, streams spill their banks and pour into fast-flowing rivers. Finally the flood empties into the sea. But not all freshwater follows such a direct path.

In places, such as on the south Devon coast, a barrier to the sea has formed. A massive shingle ridge stretches some 3.5 kilometres along the length of Start Bay. Inland lies Slapton Ley, the largest area of freshwater to be found along the Channel coast, and the largest natural lake in south-west England. It is managed as a nature reserve by the Field Studies Centre. Including the woodland, swamp, marsh and open water, which seldom averages more than a couple of metres deep, the ley covers an area of some 188 hectares. The area is divided into two parts: the dense reed-covered higher ley to the north, into which access by people is strictly controlled, and the larger open-water lower ley to the south. Each year hundreds of students and visitors walk the nature trail that winds along the landward side of the lower ley.

The calm freshwaters of Slapton Ley lap gently on the shore and the trickling streams that are its source run in all but the driest weather, keeping its water fresh despite the close proximity of the sea. Salt spray and the occasional winter surf reaching across the ridge are soon diluted and flushed from the ley. Its only outflow passes down a short fall and into the darkness of a culvert cut beneath the tiny village of Torcross at its southern end.

The flow of freshwater from the ley is never constant. It may flood after rain and dry completely during a drought. Storms and easterly winds can move tonnes of shingle in a single tide, blocking the outfall and causing the water levels in the ley to rise. Another tide and another wind, and the pressure of water behind pushes a new stream through the shingle. Occasionally human help is required, and mechanical diggers are brought in to clear a way. At other times the overflow is so great and the water pouring in a raging torrent so strong, that any creatures caught in its flood are washed into the sea. The outflow is also an entrance for some creatures that use it to gain access from the sea to the sheltered waters of the ley.

In the last week in April, conditions are right for an annual invasion of wriggling young eels. Although barely 65 millimetres in length when they reach British shores, they have already travelled some 7000 kilometres crossing the Atlantic Ocean from their place of birth somewhere in the depths of the Sargasso Sea. Their feat of navigation remains one of the most impressive and mysterious in nature.

En route the larval eels have become elvers, resembling miniature adults, and it is then that their European invasion begins. Some pass through the Strait of Gibraltar and into the Mediterranean, others enter the northern waters of the Baltic, and the rest advance on the west coast of Britain and into the English Channel. All the countless millions of elvers on the move are driven by the urge to find freshwater. They stream into estuaries or continue along the coast, sensing the flows pouring out of smaller rivers and streams. A spring tide, warm light winds and a dark night are the best conditions for elvers to begin their freshwater assault. While the females travel considerable distances, the males do not go as far upstream. Both keep close to the banks and avoid the fastest flowing currents. By day they hide in the mud and sand near the river's edge waiting for the cover of dark. When the outfall is in full flood at Slapton, it seems impossible that such tiny creatures could progress against the flow. Yet in the current-soaked shingle near the entrance to the culvert, hundreds of elvers lurk between the pebbles, waiting for slack water at the height of the tide. As the last rays of sun leave the beach and the waves are lapping at the outfall entrance, a torchlight reveals a long sinuous line of elvers disappearing into the culvert. At the far end lies the elvers' last hurdle – a weir, where the water from the ley spills over the lip and down the short slope in shallow fast running streams. Climbing this is a race against time, because as the tide retreats again the height of the weir will increase. Seeking out the gentlest flows and trickles, the intertwining silvery strings wind and wriggle their way up to the level of the ley. The main mass moves overnight. However, when the first light of dawn breaks in the east, stragglers can still be seen working their way up between cracks and resting among the fine algal growth that carpets the fall.

In the light of day elvers are easy pickings for predators. A kingfisher plunges the shallows for breakfast, while herons lurch frantically for meagre morsels as some of the late elvers struggle over the lip of the weir into the muddy depths of the ley. Others avoid waterfalls and cascading streams by wriggling up alongside in the sodden vegetation. Elvers are sensitive to the slightest flow of water and so at first, many make their way into the feeder streams. After a few months in freshwater they begin to eat and grow again, but their urge to wander remains. During winter, as the streams grow colder, they return to the warmer depths of the ley. Their formerly transparent bodies become pigmented, yellow on the back and sides, and oval scales begin to grow embedded in their skin. Their eyes are small behind the rather broad snout and the colour of the soft body gradually changes to darker grey on the back.

Like the adults, the young growing eels are distinctly nocturnal. They feed on insect larvae, shellfish, smaller fish, frogs and snails, steadily growing in size and appetite over the next few years. The eels that spend much of their time in the ley are thought to consume large quantities of fish eggs and small fry, and may in the past have contributed to a crash in the number of fish that inhabited its water. Then eels started being netted on a regular basis. At first they were caught in their hundreds but after a few seasons the catches steadily declined. This was followed in recent years by an explosion in the population of small fish in the ley.

In early spring, thousands of roach and rudd now shoal in the warming shallows. Spawning takes place near the banks on a stony bottom or over dense submerged weed. Up to 100 000 eggs are produced by each female, and they hatch between four to ten days after laying, depending on the water's warmth. Warm water is also thought to increase the young's metabolism and subsequent growth. At barely 6 millimetres in length, the hatchlings are vulnerable to other larger fish and so keep to shallow water and denser weed, feasting on microscopic plants and animals. Among the threats in open water are perch and young pike, both of which feed by day on the fry of other fish and are common in the ley. Mature pike and perch migrate into the higher ley to spawn in early spring, although pike also seem to spawn near Torcross in the lower ley.

43

Left: *The coastal village of Torcross lies at the southern-most end of Slapton Ley. This large reed fringed area of open water is known as the Lower Ley.*

Above, top: *From the north, the shingle ridge, stretching the length of Start Bay, was formed slowly at the end of the last ice age. The beach that once lay further out in the Channel was washed inland by rising seas.*

Below: *Elvers struggle up the weir that leads into the ley. The final stage of a journey which brought them across the Atlantic, along the Channel coast and into this freshwater outflow.*

Birds, too, begin to breed at this time. One of the most numerous is the coot, a waterbird very much at home on large open stretches of water. In contrast, the closely related moorhen keeps more to the cover of the ley's extensive reedbeds and shallows. The waterbird population swells during winter, when some 3000 coots have been counted on the ley. Frequently, large numbers of tufted duck, mallard, teal, widgeon and a few pairs of goldeneye can also be found. As summer approaches the number of waterbirds and wildfowl decline, and by late spring the coot population is reduced to some fifty resident breeding pairs.

Fringing the large expanse of open water the broad swaying reedbeds afford good cover for breeding birds, from the smallest warbler to the biggest swan. The nest of the mute swan consists of a huge pile of plant material befitting a bird of such grand stature. Both sexes build the nest. The male, known as a cob, collects pieces of reeds and weeds, and the female, known as a pen, heaps these into a platform with a shallow depression in the top. Here she lays between five and seven large grey-green eggs which take up to thirty-eight days to hatch. During this period the male is fiercely territorial, aggressively defending his lifelong mate from disturbance by other swans, people or dogs. Mute swans are not as silent as their name implies, and will snort and hiss loudly when annoyed.

Swan courtship is a relatively sedate affair, far removed from the complex and energetic antics of some other ley dwellers, the great crested grebes. They start pairing from late winter, performing a courtship that involves one of the bird world's most ritualised displays. The ceremony may once have provided proof of a bird's fitness to be a mate. Today it has evolved into an elaborate series of symbolic gestures but still serves a purpose, reinforcing the pair's bonding and keeping them together until nesting begins. Both male and female can play identical parts, and the birds look so much alike that presumably only grebes can reliably tell each other apart. During their display, they move through distinctive stages, like the steps in a dance, each of which has been given a name.

When looking for a mate, single grebes call attention to themselves with a croaking call that carries far across the water. On meeting, a potential partner approaches in a shallow 'ripple dive' before rising to stand tall in the water, in the so-called 'ghostly penguin display'. The second bird faces it in the 'cat display' with the head held low, neck and head feathers fanned and wings tilted forwards, and then both head-shake together. There are several different stages before they reach the full head-shaking display which starts with the pair meeting head down in threatening posture. As heads rise with feathers fanned, they shake their down-pointed bills from side to side uttering a 'ticking' call.

Once heads are held high, they alternately waggle and sway until one or both begin 'habit preening' – turning the head away to flick a feather on the back. After head shaking, the birds dive to collect some weed, and then surface and swim towards each other. They rise breast to breast with vigorously paddling feet and sway bills laden with trailing weed from side to side in the 'penguin display'.

During the grebes' head-shaking ceremony, one of the birds may suddenly dash away, 'patter flying' across the water in front of its mate. The fleeing bird then drops into the 'cat display', pauses and turns once more to face its mate, which may partially mirror its partners' wing-tilting stance. More practical than the elaborate postures and flamboyant displays is the offering by the male of a courtship gift. Instead of the symbolic flag-waving strands of weed, it is a small fish for her to eat.

The nest of the great crested grebe is usually a floating raft of weed anchored to some nearby plants. Up to five eggs are laid and the parents take it in turn to sit on them. During the twenty-eight day incubation period, the clean white shells become soiled and stained by the water weeds upon which they rest. After hatching, the attractively striped young keep close to their parents because danger lurks among the reeds in the form of mink, and beneath the surface from pike.

The largest predatory fish found in Britain's freshwater, pike grow up to a metre in length. These powerful hunters prey on other fish, including their own kind, and on small waterbirds. Grebes are especially vulnerable when very young, and pike are masters of the surprise attack. They wait for a passing meal, manoeuvring slowly, only the pectoral fins occasionally fanning, with their long green body concealed in the weed. As young birds follow their parents close to the reeds, a pike hidden below can clearly see the chicks against the brightness of the sky. With a powerful movement of the big muscular tail, its streamlined body surges forward. Only the sudden disappearance of the last chick in line and a ring of rippling water betrays the fish's deadly silent move.

Pike are not always successful. Adult grebes are accomplished divers, chasing and catching small fish, and so are likely to spot an aquatic predator. In addition, the behaviour of great crested grebes in pike-infested waters helps ensure the survival of more young. When the chicks leave the nest soon after hatching, their parents allow them to climb on to their backs and ride in comfort and safety. This strategy begins even earlier, when the grebes shelter the brooding young amongst the warm dry feathers on their backs in their wet, floating raft of a nest. Slapton Ley now supports around five resident pairs of great crested

Top: *A pike lurks motionless among the weed waiting for passing prey. They can be seen in the shallows of the lagoon.*

Above: *A dragonfly newly emerged is soft and vulnerable at first. It will be an hour or more before its wings and body are hard enough to fly.*

Right: *Distinguished by its pale eyebrow, the sedge warbler builds a nest which is usually well hidden and low down in dense vegetation.*

48

grebe, which are the cause of much local interest. Although these grebes are not uncommon in eastern Britain, in Slapton Ley they are at the very western limit of their range.

In early summer, a growing jungle of reed fringes the open water and crowds the higher ley. Swaying in the lightest breeze their tall stems form a dense flooded forest, difficult to penetrate on foot but easily accessible from the air. The first chattering swallows, newly returned from Africa, dive overhead and skim low across the water, greedily scooping insects from the air. Just as vocal but not so easily seen are the migrant warblers that breed in the reserve, having also wintered south of the Sahara. The aptly named reed warbler is probably the most common and, along with the sketchy song of the sedge warbler, adds to the gentle summer sound of wind-rustled reeds.

The warbler's nest, mainly built by the female, is a well-hidden cup of long leaves carefully woven around a few stiff stems. Flexible but firm, the structure can sway with the reeds yet support up to five young birds in the case of the reed warbler or six of the sedge. Adult warblers move easily through the towering leaf-draped stands, sidling up and down the reeds, and hopping from stem to stem. The skulking behaviour of these birds in their sun-dappled world, deep inside the reedbed, is not without danger, especially when sitting on eggs. Both reed and sedge warblers frequently fall victim to the female cuckoo. If they escape becoming unwitting foster parents to a cuckoo's offspring, reed warblers can rear their young in about eleven to twelve days from hatching. The adults are kept busy feeding their growing band of young with a rich assortment of the small insect life that thrives around the ley.

Less frequently heard are the distant reeling call of the grasshopper warbler and, in marked contrast, the explosive staccato song of the rare cetti's warbler. The cetti's astonishingly loud call, emanating from a dense patch of reed, startles human visitors and can carry far across the ley. Unlike the other warblers, it is resident throughout the year and is a relative newcomer to the reserve, having been first recorded in 1974 and not confirmed as breeding for another two years. It is now known that the ley supports thirty-seven singing males and each one may have more than one mate, so perhaps many more nests.

As the weather warms, the plant life of the ley thrives. The presence of the field study centre allows many students and researchers to monitor and measure the quality of the water and the life that it supports. The ley is a nutrient-rich lake with additional contributions of phosphates coming from Slapton sewage works, and nitrates from adjacent agricultural land. As a result the growth of some plant life is more lush than in other lakes. Indeed, waterways can become

Far left: *Hot and dry during summer the shingle ridge is a harsh place for plants to survive. Blue viper's bugloss, sea carrot and sea spurge are some of the few that can thrive.*

Above: *The yellow horned poppy is one of the most attractive flowers to be found on the seaward side of the shingle ridge.*

Left: *Water lilies emerge from the ley in summer. Their floating leaves provide vital shade for fish and other aquatic life.*

choked with rank vegetation and increased algal growth, leading to the shading of other plants below and the subsequent decrease of fish life.

The minute single-celled green and blue-green algae that flourish in the surface waters are a plentiful source of food for young growing fish. But in some especially hot years, after weeks of clear cloudless skies, the algal bloom is so prolific that a wind-pushed tide of bright green algae is washed into the shallows and deposited on the shores of the ley. In recent summers, as elsewhere, these blooms have been found to be potentially toxic. They contain large quantities of a blue-green microcystis algae in concentrations sufficient to kill farm stock or dogs allowed to drink the waters where toxins accumulate. Notices warn visitors and fishermen at this time to keep clear. Within a few weeks, the vigour of the bloom subsides, the wind disperses the algae once more, and the danger passes. These events are being closely monitored, and research suggests a significant link with the increasing use of fertilisers on surrounding farmland. The results of the study should benefit both the reserve and the farmers who are wasting valuable fertilisers which get washed into the ley. Farming also brings benefits. The trampling by cattle coming down to drink has produced the ideal conditions for a special flower to grow. The strapwort, one of the rarest and most inconspicuous plants in Britain, is now known to survive only at Slapton Ley.

Below the algae-strewn surface, diving beetles and wandering snails, nymphs and the larvae of flying insects tempt student pond-dippers to explore another world. Above flutter the damselflies, which include the delicate common blue, azure and elegant blue-tailed, resting amongst the lush waterside vegetation. Stronger flying hawker and darter dragonflies skim the surface in pursuit of other insect prey or a mate. Between the reeds, flamboyant yellow irises shine in the early morning light and patches of forget-me-not colour the sodden soil. In the shallows a mass of water crowfoot opens its white buttercup-like flowers to the sun. Further out, lily pads pushed up from the depths, float in rafts on the surface. These plants of the damp margins and flooded ground are water dwellers and cannot endure prolonged periods of desiccation. The plants of the arid, windswept shore nearby require different features to survive where the baking sun sucks the shingle dry and the constant breeze deposits salt spray. They have thick fleshy leaves and stems, deep searching taproots and an ability to cope with the shifting shingle on this exposed crest of the shore.

Throughout the summer, a colourful succession of flowers on the shore marks the passage of the seasons. The top of the ridge boasts a relatively sparse cover of green, tenaciously clinging to the thin deposits of humus trapped between the growth. It is a harsh place to live and the pioneering plants closest to the sea face the most severe conditions. Looking almost out of place, the paper thin petals of the yellow horned poppy shake in the wind. Its name comes from the long, curved seed pods it produces, which reach up to 30 centimetres in length. In late summer these split open to release a cargo of seeds to be scattered widely along the ridge. Deep in the shingle, they survive the winter surf and raging storms which may destroy the older plants. In spring a small rosette of leaves appears which can survive from year to year. The tough, waxy and hairy leaves are well adapted to reduce water loss and a long root reaches fresh moisture deep down. From midsummer, each rosette produces a mass of tall flowering stems which can grow up to 90 centimetres high.

Thriving alongside the yellow horned poppy is the ancestor of a cultivated vegetable, the sea radish. It has a deep tap root that is longer, thinner and more woody than its plump garden relative. Another plant whose relative is well known is the sea carrot. Unlike its vegetable cousin it has a small tap root, but its leaves do have the distinctive smell of carrot and its tiny flowers are arranged in a characteristic large flat-topped umbel. One wild plant found on the ridge that was once commonly eaten by people is scurvy grass. It is not actually a grass, but a small flowered plant with fleshy heart-shaped leaves rich in vitamin C. This made it an important supplement for sailors trying to ward off the effects of scurvy. Other pioneers are the green sea spurge and white-flowered sea campion. The ridge also sports many maritime plants including clumps of thrift or sea pink, the daisy flowered sea mayweed and even the occasional rare sea holly.

The grinding movement of shingle on the beach ensures a constant supply of lime from the broken sea shells cast up on to the shore. Thriving in these soils is a plant with a striking flower. Its developing buds turn from pink to purple, finally becoming blue when they burst open. Then from each flower the female stigma protrudes beyond the petals, forking at the end like a snake's tongue. This has given rise to the plant's common name, viper's bugloss.

The plant community growing along the shingle ridge is able to weather most of the vagaries of wind and tide, shifting shingle and drought, yet it is incredibly fragile. And on its survival depend not only individual flowers but the very future of the ley. Trampling feet and car tyres quickly destroy the thin layer of turf, allowing winter storms to erode and breach the ridge, and destroy the ley's only sea defence.

In the past, the shore has been the scene of another type of death and destruction. During the Second World War, American forces used Slapton Sands to prepare and practise for the allied invasion of France in 1944. Sadly one of the rehearsals went disastrously wrong when the troops were surprised by fast-moving German torpedo boats. They sank two American tank landing ships and over 700 men were drowned. Indeed many more American lives were lost that day than during the actual D-Day landings themselves. Walking now along the beach on a warm summer's day, a gentle breeze disturbing the flowers and a sparkling blue sea beyond, it is difficult to imagine Slapton Sands as a battleground. The only reminder and memorial to that fateful hour is a solitary Sherman tank raised from the seabed and sited as a monument near Torcross.

In an effort to protect the ridge, a road has been built along its length which helps strengthen the shingle bank and three well-spaced car parks reduce damage to the flora between. The car park at Torcross also gives access to the public bird hide overlooking the ley. Along the landward side, the back of the ridge is dominated by thickets of bramble and gorse where many small birds forage and breed. The frequent hovering kestrel and the occasional wheeling silhouette of a larger buzzard are useful indicators to the presence of small mammals along this stretch.

In late summer, after several weeks with little or no rain, the water level in the ley begins to drop. The muddy margins and gravel shores are exposed and new height is given to the surrounding reeds. The outfall no longer flows, the weir dries in the baking sun and fish gather in the shallows in even greater numbers. As the depth of water decreases so too does the apparent size of the fish. In the warmest parts, nearest to the shore, this year's spawning of tiny silver shapes crowd the waterweed. The shoals appear to be sorted by size, mingling and moving amongst their own kind. In the watery world of fish, there is safety in numbers. They scatter at the slightest shadow or sudden movement, and a patrolling pike, well fed on an abundance of prey, causes a sudden wave of panic to ripple across the surface. The parting shoals mark its stealthy progress.

A kingfisher perched on a bent reed watches intently as a shoal moves in its direction. Suddenly it plunges headlong towards a single fish picked from the teeming shapes below. The bird takes little more than a second to enter the water, catch its prey and leave the surface in a flurry of wings and spray. Seen in slow motion, the flash of blue and gold rises phoenix-like from a crown of water, its quarry firmly gripped in its beak or, sometimes, impaled. Flying to a more substantial branch the kingfisher stuns its prey with a deft flick of the beak against its perch, before swallowing the fish head first. The majority of its prey is small, the largest, up to 8 centimetres, being actually about half its

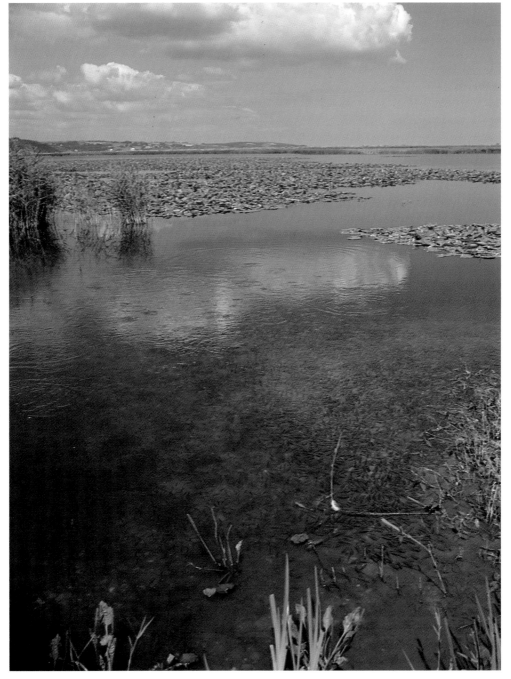

Huge shoals of roach and rudd gather in the warmth of the shallows. Fish grow faster in warm water and the smallest come close to the edge of the lagoon.

length, and it may eat fifteen or more fish a day. If there is no overhanging perch from which to launch an attack, kingfishers can hover. In deeper water the birds need to dive from quite a height to plunge just 25 centimetres. Any fish below this are generally out of reach.

A different fishing method is employed by the large grey heron. Walking carefully into the shallows, or alighting on some matted growth further out in the ley, it watches and waits. A long neck and dagger-like beak provide the power and tool for the job. Gradually, shoals of larger fish move within reach and a lightning strike grasps or spears the prey. At one time herons used to breed at Slapton but today the nearest heronry is several miles away to the north, on the Dart estuary. There are now plenty of fish in the ley to support herons, kingfishers and diving grebes, all feeding in different ways on the same stretch of water. The increasing number of cormorants is another good indication of the thriving piscine population.

Perhaps one of the most unlikely predators of small fish is the grass snake. An able undulating swimmer in open water, the grass snake moves effortlessly through the tangled forest of reed stems and aquatic weeds which dominate the ley's margins. It is a harmless snake, incapable of hurting people except for a foul smell produced when frightened or roughly handled. The adder, however, is Britain's only venomous snake and should be treated with due respect. It is only occasionally encountered in the quietest parts of the reserve and rarer still out on the shingle ridge.

The ley also caters for human fishermen who wish to while away the hours in peace and quiet with a rod and line. A few boats for hire from the field centre give fishermen their only opportunity to explore the ley at leisure and seek out the best catches. These people are not, however, the only mammals in pursuit of fish prey. The ubiquitous mink, a fur-farm escapee now living in the wild, has a more varied diet that includes fish. In captivity the once much-sought-after coat of the mink was bred in a variety of colours. Today the fashion among their free-living offspring is a reversion to the original wild fur that is dark brown, almost black.

Wild mink are now common, and the results of a major study at Slapton go some way to explain their apparent success. Although mink are accomplished swimmers, fish make up at most some 60 per cent of their diet, and at the least, only 20 per cent. The rest comprises large numbers of moorhens, coots and ducks. Elsewhere they also take large numbers of rabbits, voles and rats. The wild mink can be surprisingly bold, foraging along the water's edge in broad daylight. Indeed one young mink, while inquisitively searching around the boats and beneath the wooden jetty, actually ran under my feet! As well as being flexible in their diet, mink are prolific. They can produce five to six young in a single litter, and these are weaned at eight weeks, attain adult size in four months and breed themselves the following spring.

The first record of mink breeding in the wild came in 1956 from the upper reaches of the Teign in Devon. Since then they have spread across most of southern England. Subsequent escapes have firmly established the mink as a new and unwelcome addition to Britain's predatory fauna. The increasing population of mink was once thought to be a major threat to the most famous resident at Slapton Ley, the native British otter. However, contrary to popular opinion, these two related creatures seem to compete little over food. Although there is an overlap in their diet, fish were found to be three times as important to otters, and at Slapton, the otters take a much higher proportion of roach, eel and pike than mink. In summer, particularly, when large fish are traditionally more difficult to catch, the otter is more accomplished at taking this prey, while the mink turns its attention to the seasonal glut of birds and small mammals on land. The otter also has one major advantage – size. An adult female otter weighs three to four times more than a fully grown male mink, and so would be more than a match for it in direct confrontation.

While mink have spread across the country despite the presence of people, the otter is intolerant of disturbance and so seeks out the few remaining backwaters that remain quiet and free from human beings. The wilderness of overgrown, wind-rustling reed that is the higher ley is bisected only by a narrow channel. This passes between towering stems, which in places threaten to engulf the route and in others widen into deep dark pools. Beyond lies the ley's greatest asset, the swamp, which remains impenetrable to people but accessible to the otter.

It is fortunate, though not unknown, to see wild otters at Slapton, but very rare to catch more than a mere glimpse. They are incredibly shy, move mainly by night and are wary of the slightest hint of danger. Their prowess underwater is shown by their lithe antics as they swoop after fish, diving and turning in tight circles. A streamlined shape and the lack of external ears aid smooth motion through the water, and both ears and nostrils can be closed. Their swimming is in two modes. The 'dog' paddle, using all four feet, provides a progress on the surface that is relatively slow but sustainable for long periods if necessary. High speed comes from undulating the entire body. The forepaws are held tight to the chest, except when changing direction, while the hind legs that trail sole upwards and the flattened tail provide the main thrust.

Left: *The higher ley lies at the northern end of the nature reserve and is closed to the public.*

Left: *A young heron finds easy pickings among the eels and other fish of the lagoon.*

Below: *Grass snakes are harmless to people as they lack any venom. The forked tongue is used to scent the air and ground.*

Below: *A fish's eye view of a hunting grass snake. They are good swimmers.*

The eyesight of the otter is good on land and excellent underwater. Unlike us, who have clear vision only when the surface of the eye is in contact with air, otters can change the shape of their lens, making it more spherical to cope with the different refractive index of water. In dark, murky water, tactile facial hairs become the principal bristling sense for finding food. The otter's energetic pace of life requires regular feeding. At Slapton, its staple diet varies with the season, eels being caught and eaten in greater quantities during the summer months, and roach being the main winter diet. This may be due to the eel's habit of hiding in the mud during cold weather. Roach, on the other hand, are active all year and as water temperatures rise in summer they tend to gather in fast-moving shoals. Although superbly adapted to its semi-aquatic life, the European otter usually spends less than one minute underwater before having to surface for air. When alarmed and attempting to escape from danger, dives of up to four minutes have been recorded, but these are thought to be exceptional.

On land the otters' bounding gait gives them a fair turn of speed, as fast as a human athlete over short distances. They frequent well-used tracks and are not averse to using steep slopes as a mud slide. But apart from the occasional tantalising footprint known, confusingly, as a 'seal', the most regular signs of otters are their droppings or sprains. It is now known that these are not just territorial markers but a complex chemical signature containing traces of proteins and sugars produced by special glands. A single stone at the edge of the water may contain several different sprains, and each one carries its owner's unique chemical fingerprint. Compared with our own sadly inadequate olfactory abilities, those of the otter are acute. A close investigation and good sniff can reveal details of an individual, which probably include its age, sex and the time of its last visit. The approach of a person or another otter is likely to be signalled by sound as well as smell. Each night otters roam up to several kilometres at a time, swimming or running along the bank, stopping to investigate every strange smell and listening intently to any sounds that pierce the dark. The actual size of an individual's territory is affected by the availability of food, and each range will include good sources. Slapton Ley is highly productive with plenty of dense cover offering an abundance of prey in a relatively small area. Consequently, otters here have no need to cover great distances in the search for a meal. Although otters are mainly solitary animals, they do have a hierarchy, and location of a home range also depends on status and sex. The most dominant male holds the best located and largest territory, which may overlap those of more than one female. This is because while a female only needs a single mate to produce successful young, a male otter can increase the number of his offspring by mating with more than one female. The bigger his territory, the more females he can monopolise, but there are of course limits. Each otter's share of the ley must be regularly patrolled and marked in order to protect the valuable site from intrusion by another of its own kind. A large territory is more difficult to defend, and the more females it contains the more attractive it becomes to other males.

Another important requirement for an otter is a variety of resting places. Most are in thick vegetation or well hidden under a pile of branches. More permanent are the tunnels dug between boulders or tangled tree roots in the banks of a stream or at the back of the ley. These dens or holts are often the enlarged diggings of other animals, and provide a safe retreat especially for a female with cubs. Females are particular when choosing a site for breeding, and pick the most inaccessible and least likely to be disturbed place in their territory.

In Britain, otters breed at almost any time of the year but many young are born in spring or early summer. The breeding holt may lie deep under the protective roots of a tree, out in dense woodland or in the middle of a reedbed. Shortly before birth the female furnishes her nest with a bulky ball of bedding, and a hollow in the centre forms the nursery for the first few weeks. Here, in safety and darkness, she gives birth, to usually two or three cubs or, more rarely, up to five. We know from the intimate studies of two litters that, at birth, the cubs are 15 centimetres long, blind, toothless and squeak loudly. Their bodies are covered in a velvety fine mouse-grey fur and they are quite helpless at first. After twelve days or so they begin to crawl, their eyes open after thirty-one days and they begin eating solid food at around forty-nine days old. Suckling continues up to sixty-nine days, and they enter the water for the first time about three days later. By then, the young cubs have grown the dense waterproof coat of their parents, but will remain with their mother for up to a year.

All otters are vocal, and the cubs particularly so. They play noisily, a constant chatter of high-pitched piping and whickering accompanying their boisterous antics and the occasional pint-sized threat. Adults maintain contact with each other using a short chirp or a one-second-long, ear piercing whistle. When apprehensive or threatened a low growl or explosive 'hah' gives vent to their anger or fright, while in appeasement the note is a more conciliatory low-pitched twitter.

Otters face many hazards. In the past they were hunted extensively and so it is not surprising that it was the hunters who first noticed the decline in their population during the early 1960s. It was soon realised that this was no local incident, but a country-wide crash that was among the first warning signs of the build-up of lethal toxins in the environment. The cause was eventually traced to the reckless use of organochlorine pesticides, especially dieldrin, which was employed extensively for sheep dipping and seed dressing. This highly persistent pesticide washed from the land through the soil and into the waterways. Here the chemical was taken up by microscopic organisms, which were eaten by small water animals and they, in turn, were preyed on by fish. The chemical became more and more concentrated as it passed through the food chain which culminated in the otter. Throughout southern England the otters that for centuries had hunted the rivers and streams of the lowlands disappeared.

Restrictions on the extensive and uncontrolled use of pesticides were applied too late for many regions of the country. Southern and central England lost virtually their entire otter population, and only in Scotland, Wales, Norfolk and the south-west of England did the otter survive. Following the first controls on pesticide use, a brief rise in otter numbers promised a recovery, but they never managed to reclaim lost ground. They had been reduced to a pathetically small population, spread too far and too thin. During the years that followed the crash, urban development, increasing disturbance and the systematic clearing of river banks, all took their toll on the already depleted numbers. Other pollutants too, such as the heavy metals mercury and lead, continued to turn up in fish, and their effect on the otter was incalculable.

Early campaigns to save the otter attracted public attention, and conservation bodies joined the growing demand for legislation to protect the surviving population. However, it was not until January 1978 that the otter in England and Wales finally became fully protected by law. The introduction of the 1982 Countryside and Wildlife Act extended protection to Scottish otters as well. Today their biggest threats are disturbance and loss of suitable habitat. In addition, some otters are still illegally shot by fishing interests or killed accidentally on roads or drowned in lobster pots. Despite such losses, the otter continues to maintain a stronghold in Devon and Cornwall, and those at Slapton Ley play an important part in this. Precautions taken here minimise the risks, for example, eel traps contain special guards with an entrance hole too small for an otter to pass through.

The long hot days of summer at Slapton end abruptly as wind and heavy rain lash the reeds and make the water boil. Each drop renews the life blood of the ley. Its level, lowered by weeks of drought, begins to rise and the weir flows once more. September brings twittering flocks of swallows to the ley, which

The European otter is a shy and normally nocturnal animal. Only in the more remote parts of the country do they appear by day and the south-west of England remains a stronghold.

skim low over the water to scoop the last glut of flying insects into their gapes. Only sunset brings a temporary lull in their activity, as increasing numbers arrive to roost in the safety of the reedbeds. These are passage migrants, stopping a few days to replenish their supplies before continuing south. The shorter days and cooler nights bring in other migrants, less obvious than the swallows but similarly en route to warmer climes. Ahead of them lies the widest part of the English Channel, southern Europe and the dry expanse of the Sahara. Each autumn and spring many of these small birds are caught, ringed and released unharmed to continue their biannual odyssey. The records reveal that chiffchaffs and warblers, though small and lightweight, are capable of covering thousands of kilometres to escape the harsh northern winters.

In autumn, the reedbeds begin to lose colour, turning from lush green to pale straw, and other birds arrive for a longer stay. Compared to the rest of Europe, Slapton Ley has a mild climate, with rare frosts that seldom last long. This attracts hundreds of wildfowl, including widgeon, teal and tufted duck, to winter in the reserve. Autumn brings other highlights each year for the growing numbers of people interested in watching birds. Osprey, bittern and harriers all make regular appearances. Even purple herons can occasionally be seen and wintering bearded tits are recorded in most years.

For sheer spectacle and overwhelming numbers nothing can beat the sight on a clear winter's eve of the starlings. Each winter vast numbers of starlings arrive from northern Europe to swell the population of our resident British birds. By late afternoon, small flocks of these common birds have already been flying in for an hour or so to pitch in an adjacent field or on the bare branches of an old oak tree. As the sun begins to set the volume of chatter coming from the birds in the field gives a clue to their numbers, but it is not until they lift off in a frenzy of wings that the scale of their gathering becomes apparent.

Starlings are highly gregarious birds and feed in flocks out in a field, seldom fighting because there is plenty of space. Gathering together also has the advantage of greatly reducing the chances of an individual being caught by a predator. When feeding, a bird must divide its time between pecking, probing, walking and watching. In a flock less time needs to be spent looking out for danger. The bigger the flock, the less each needs to watch and the more time individuals have to find food. At dusk several of these feeding flocks come together and such a gathering can sometimes number hundreds of thousands of birds. Throughout the year starlings sleep in communal roosts, but it is in winter when they gather in the biggest flocks that they are most noticeable. Groups may come from up to 30 kilometres away, small flocks merging en route and joining others at the pre-roost assembly. There is much activity as feathers must be cleaned and conditioned through preening and washing at the end of the day. The assembly places change periodically, making the starlings less vulnerable to predators. The resting places, however, are predictable, and short-eared owl, hen harrier, kestrel, sparrowhawk and peregrine are all known to take starlings coming into roost.

The starlings take off together and travel en masse to the roost, but the flight is seldom direct. If wind and weather conditions are calm, the birds will indulge in one of the extravagant wonders of the bird world. A complex series of co-ordinated movements results in a cloud-like formation climbing and wheeling in the evening sky. In the swirling mass, individuals seem to move as one. How the birds turn without colliding into each other has intrigued people for centuries. Careful study has shown that the birds do not move as a single unit as if from a central command. Changes of direction flow through the flock. Yet, although the reaction time of a small bird is quick, the changes seem to flow too fast for a bird simply to be reacting to its immediate neighbour. Each turn appears to emanate from one edge of the flock, and the birds on the inside are thought to see the move begin some way off and so anticipate when their turn comes. In this way the speed of any change is accelerated and the flock moves through the evening air as if performing a well-rehearsed aerial display. The favoured roost is out in one of the reedbeds. As the sun dips below the surrounding hills the starlings fly low over the reeds, seemingly continuing their fly past. Suddenly they turn and drop from the air into the safety of the stems. With the fading light the chattering crescendo slowly subsides and darkness envelops the ley.

In time the season turns, the starlings and other winter visitors depart, and the return of longer warmer days brings new growth. Nothing in nature is constant. In terms of landscape lakes are temporary features and Slapton's pure lagoon is no exception. It has survived for perhaps no more than a few thousand years and even now is shrinking. Sediments washed in by streams, and soil from the surrounding hills, are gradually silting up the shallows. As the deeper parts get within reach of the sunlight, plants take root. Reedbeds slowly spread from the margins encroaching on the open water. Roots, leaves and stems rot, and the decaying vegetation adds to the deposits. So in turn the lake becomes a swamp, then a marsh, a meadow and finally a wood. But with careful management, some of the growth can be controlled, water levels maintained and Slapton Ley can continue as a haven for wildlife, just a stone's throw from the sea.

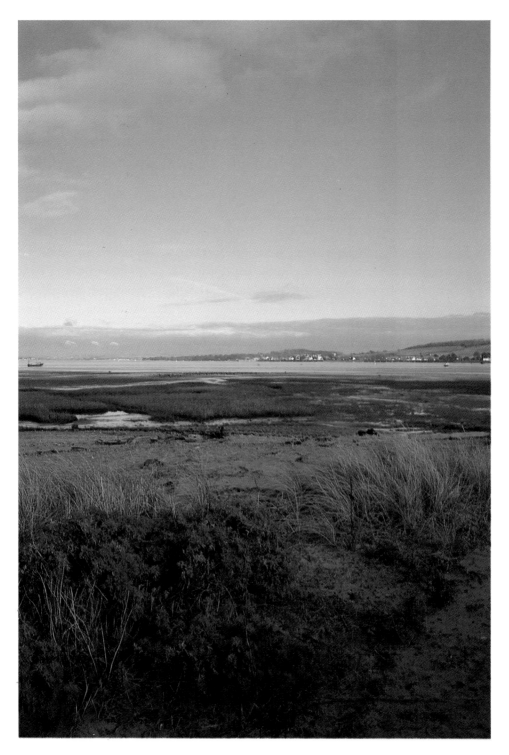

The Exe estuary is internationally important for its wildlife. It is one of only 36 estuaries in Britain to hold over 20 000 wildfowl and wading birds.

CHAPTER THREE

Turn of the Tide

*T*HERE ARE FEW places in Europe where the coastline is not in retreat and even fewer where the land advances at the expense of the sea. One such is the Exe estuary which lies in a drowned river valley bordering the southern shore of Britain. All rivers contain sediment by the time they reach the coast. Even the clearest waters carry mineral particles and decayed organic matter too small for the human eye to perceive. Turbid waters contain tonnes of such material and seasonal floods load them even more. As the river Exe nears the shore, fresh water meets salt and its flow falters and spreads. The sediments form bigger particles, clump together and gradually settle to form vast expanses of mud at the mouth of the river. Twice a day, this estuary's huge banks and meandering channels are flooded by the incoming tide, and twice left exposed.

In terms of wildlife and scenic beauty, the Exe is one of the largest and most important estuaries emptying into the Channel. Its source lies high on the windswept hills of Exmoor and its waters are swelled by several tributaries traversing rich Devon soil. All add to the load of fine silt deposited at the river's mouth. Estuarine mud has a distinct character. If you wade out on to the flats at low tide, the fineness will suck at your boots. If you pick up a handful, the smooth-grained stickiness will ooze through your clenched fingers. Disturbing the underlying black layer with foot or spade sends up the whiff of hydrogen sulphide – rotten eggs. So smooth is the mud that this and other gases produced by the bacterial decay of organic material are trapped beneath the surface.

The surface of the smelly mud is a harsh place for plants and animals. In winter it can be bleak and swept by freezing winds, and in summer baked and dry. Twice daily the water which flows over the mud changes dramatically in its make-up. When the tide is outgoing the estuary water is fresh, especially when the river is in full spate and swollen by rain. The return of the tide brings a flood of salt water. In between, the vast expanses of mud are uncovered and exposed to the air. It may seem unlikely that any creatures could endure such extreme conditions, yet some do and they thrive, for the benefits are great.

Regular supplies of food are delivered by both river and sea, giving this habitat the potential of being among the richest on earth. In addition, the creatures that have adapted to withstand the rigours face little competition, and so are often present in huge numbers.

Bacteria and algae flourish on the mud along with other tiny organisms. In the upper reaches of the estuary, hair-like sludge worms mass where the waters are only just brackish. They consume their way head first through the surface mud while their tails wave in the oxygen-rich water above. Tolerant of pollution, they can form a fine red carpet if unchecked, swelling in numbers up to a quarter of a million in 1 square metre of mud. Down towards the sea, where the water is saltier, the estuary life is more diverse and includes hydrobia snails also known as spire shells. Each has a home little larger than a grain of wheat and 10 000 may occupy 1 square metre. Elsewhere, such as on the Tamar in Cornwall, populations of these miniature molluscs can reach five times that number. The ebbing tide exposes a tangle of tiny trails made by the snails as they plough through the surface layer, gorging on a film of diatoms and detritus. Between tides they burrow into the mud, only to reappear with the incoming tide and bob up to the surface of the water. There they are kept afloat on a mucous raft, which also traps diatoms for food, as they are carried up the estuary. They return to the lower reaches on the ebbing tide and drop back again on to the mud.

Enormous numbers of tiny shrimps, barely a centimetre long, build burrows in which to hide. Sitting safely in the entrance they sweep passing particles and other food from the water, using their hooked antennae. Although not a true shrimp, another crustacean found there is known as the opossum shrimp, or as a mysid. Opossum shrimps are abundant in estuaries and feed mainly in mid-water, especially at the edge of the incoming tide. They are named after a marsupial because the females have a brood pouch in which they carry their young. Mysids form a vital link in the food chain between smaller organisms and larger fish, young flounders being particularly partial to them.

Nearer the low-tide mark, where some sand is mixed with the mud, lugworms reveal their presence by casts and depressions. Each worm is up to 40 centimetres in length and the thickness of a little finger. It burrows beneath the surface, creating a U-shaped tube, and lines the walls of its home with mucus. It fills the tube loosely at the head end with a plug of sand grains. Then it grips the tube using short bristles on its sides and, with the piston action of a pump, draws water down through the sand. This creates a shallow pit on the surface, while below, particles of food are trapped and concentrated in the filtering plug.

After a short while pumping gives way to eating and the worm consumes the now nutritious sand. It digests the goodness and excretes the residue into the rear end of the tube. Every forty-five minutes or so, it pushes this waste up to the surface, ejecting the sand to form a cast.

The ragworm, with a line of leg-like bristles running down either side of its body, burrows at low tide in a similar way. It can tolerate lower salinity levels than the lugworm and so can exploit the sand and mud banks at higher levels where more freshwater is present. Ragworms also eat a wider range of food than lugworms. They too secrete mucus but use it to form strands which extend from the burrow into the water. A current produced by the worm draws particles of organic matter into the sticky net, and every so often the food is consumed, strands and all. In addition, ragworms are predatory, and will kill and eat other small worms.

There is one type of small, burrowing worm, just 2 centimetres long, that seems to have found a sanctuary out of reach of predators. The blushing worm is very rare, being found nowhere else in Britain. Even on the Exe estuary, it is limited to just two patches of coarse sand that are so dry they contain little dissolved oxygen. Few if any other animals can survive in such conditions, but the blushing worm apparently thrives here, some 360 having been counted in just 1 square metre. The blushing worm is a strange-looking creature, so strange that when first discovered it was described upside down and back to front. At rest, its body is blue-green or pinky white, but when burrowing, blood and body fluids are forced into the head end, making it blush and giving rise to the worm's common name. A cone-shaped organ acting as a valve builds up sufficient fluid pressure to force the head to extend and push a way through the sand.

Far more common and familiar are cockles, mussels and other bivalved molluscs, each of which has two valves or shells joined by a hinge. Several types of molluscs can live alongside each other as long as they do not compete for space. In the estuary, this can be achieved simply by living at different depths in the mud and sand. Cockles live close to the low-tide mark, where they burrow just below the surface. They feed by drawing a current of water through two raised short fleshy tubes or siphons and filtering out food particles. In favourable conditions they can occur in enormous numbers, up to 10 000 in each square metre. In contrast, mussels survive on the surface, where a tough shell and firm anchor are the only features needed to crowd out the opposition.

Mussels cannot withstand long exposure to the air and so are found only on suitable banks below the mid-tide level in the lower reaches of the Exe estuary,

Left: *Low tide at Exmouth. Twice daily throughout the year the estuary is left exposed for the birds to exploit.*

Below: *Hydrobia snail shells the size of a grain of wheat are dwarfed by the shell of a cockle. They are an important source of food for birds.*

but here they abound. They cling to the gravel surface, and each other, using bundles of sticky threads produced from a gland located on the foot. Once fixed in position, they are incapable of roaming as other molluscs do. However, some minor movement is possible by breaking threads and producing new ones. Mussels begin feeding only when covered by the incoming tide. Like cockles, they draw in water through siphons to filter out a meal, and a single mussel can pump up to 4.5 litres of water a day. It can also extend its fleshy foot to wipe any settled detritus off the outer surface of its shell. Mussels vary in size with age, and with height relative to the tide. The higher up a mussel is, the smaller it is because its feeding time is less. They breed by shedding eggs and sperm into the surrounding water, where their larvae become part of the plankton. Eventually the larvae develop into young mussels, known as spats, which settle on a suitable surface to begin the sedentary part of their lives, and may continue growing there for up to five years.

Mussels are not alone in their beds. Many other creatures live among their shells, and the tiny pea-crab even lives within the shells of living mussels. It feeds partly by intercepting food drawn in by the siphon and partly on the soft tissue of the mussel's gills. At first the female crabs can move between hosts, but become confined as they grow larger than the width of the mussel shell opening. The smaller males are not so restricted and can move readily from shell to shell to fertilise their imprisoned mates.

The outside surface of the mussel shell is sometimes encrusted by acorn barnacles. Like other barnacles, they are common around the coast and radically different from other crustaceans. Their larvae are planktonic during their first few months and grow by a series of moults, until they develop two oval shells and six pairs of legs. In this final stage of their free living existence, they are carried inshore on an advancing tide and sink to the bottom to begin a more sedentary life. They turn upside down, cement their heads to the surface and gradually undergo great change. Limy plates grow to protect the body and the legs become limbs for feeding. Here they lie, for the next few years, kicking their legs in the water and snatching at particles passing in the current. Another barnacle frequently found on mussel shells is a relative newcomer to these shores. When first described by the naturalist Charles Darwin in the nineteenth century, it was commonly found only in the estuaries of New Zealand and southern Australia. It reached European waters by hitching a lift on the hulls of ships and was first noticed in the Channel harbour of Chichester at the end of the Second World War. Since then it has spread both west to Wales and east into the North Sea.

Mussel banks also support many creatures not so permanently attached. Common edible periwinkles are grazers, roaming the beds and feeding on the surface film of algae and other growth. Related molluscs with a curious habit are the slipper limpets introduced in the 1880s with oysters from North America. They live communally in a tower of shells, one on top of the other, with the oldest at the bottom. Most members in a chain are female, the middle ones are of intermediate sex, and the youngest on top are male. Normally they live in a pile of eight or nine but a high-rise curling block can reach up to twelve. As the lower members mature and die, the upper ones grow and change sex. Unfortunately, these sedentary filter feeders have become a serious pest on oyster beds, though less so on mussel beds, because they smother them and compete for the same planktonic food. Apart from the threat of such introduced animals, mechanical damage or severe pollution, the estuary banks support a stable community of animals held together by a web of their own making.

When the tide is out, the full extent of the estuary is exposed. As can be seen from a gull's eye view soaring high above, it is not just an even spread of mud and sand. Each bank and flat, side of channel and shoreline is different. Sometimes the distinction is subtle, caused by proportions and size of silt and grain barely discernible to the eye. Currents and tides combine to produce more marked variation, providing areas where salinity and scouring limit colonisation by life, and other areas that are ideal places for particular plants and animals to thrive. This variety makes the estuary a complex patchwork of texture and colour.

On the mussel banks, the presence of grazing animals, and the cleaning of shells by the mussels themselves, give little chance for plants to become established. Similarly, few plants can colonise the other banks and flats in the lower reaches, which are scoured by wind and tide, and buried daily by new deposits of sand and silt. Seaweeds grow where they can attach their holdfast to a solid foundation, and a scattering of stones across the mud can provide all the anchorage they need. Spiral wracks survive in brackish water but bladderwracks growing in estuaries do not thrive so well and as a result have a distinctly curly form.

Between the muddiest parts of the upper estuary and the great rippled banks of sand at its mouth lies a grassy sward. This maritime meadow is produced not by seaweed but by one of the true flowering plants that have adapted to life in the sea, and the only one to do so in Britain. The perennial eel grass grows on the mud and sand flats in the more sheltered parts of the estuary towards Exmouth. Its long, grass-like leaves appear above the surface, while under-

Right: *Oystercatchers gather on the high water roost at Dawlish Warren while their feeding grounds are covered by the tide.*

Below: *Herons nest in a colony at the top of the tallest trees found alongside the estuary in the grounds of Powderham Castle.*

ground its creeping rhizomes help to stabilise the flats. Despite its appearance and name, this plant is not a grass but a relative of freshwater pondweeds. So well adapted is it to a submarine life, that even pollination occurs underwater. The flowers, having no need for petals or other fancy adornments, are enclosed in a sheath growing on a branched spike near the base. They are alternately male and female, the latter bearing tiny thread-like pollen, around 0.25 of a millimetre long. During the summer the plants, trusting to chance and the tide, release a cloudy mass of pollen that drifts through the current-bent leaves across the eel grass flats. If a pollen grain touches a narrow object it rapidly curls around, securing itself, with luck, to the protruding part of a female flower. At one time great beds of eel grass grew in the sheltered waters of most estuaries on both sides of the Atlantic. Then in 1931 a mystery disease, spreading from North America, all but wiped out the plants. The new growth is therefore relatively recent and only now is the eel grass beginning to recolonise its former flats.

The many marine creatures that lurk amongst the eel grass's leaves also suffered from its decimation. One of the most finely adapted to its linear growth is the long, narrow pipefish. Despite being relatively common in the south and west, its elongated body is not easily seen when it adopts its usual semi-vertical pose. Pipefish are closely related to sea horses and share many features with them, including incubation of the eggs by the male in a special brood pouch. Several small snails live exclusively on eel grass. Burrowing anemones and sea urchins, along with sea hares and a number of similar soft-bodied snails, all make their homes among the leaves. The loss of the plants was also acutely felt by the birds that rely on its growth in early winter, including ducks, geese and swans.

Plants are the real power behind the processes that gradually turn soft, frequently submerged mud into harder, drier ground. As the river brings down more and more sediment, and the particles bind together, the flats grow larger and higher. On the surface a slimy skin of algae (microscopic plants) begins to develop, and this starts the process of consolidation. Once the ground is firm, other plants take root and the banks grow faster. Instead of swilling around the surface and being dragged back by the tide, larger quantities of the mud particles brought by each lapping wave are trapped by the growing fabric of roots and stems. In time, the surface rises above even the highest spring tide and the life of the estuary loses out to the life on dry land.

Around European shores a plant that has pioneered the reclamation of estuaries is glasswort. This small annual with swollen translucent green stems and scale-like leaves, has the appearance of a plant surviving a drought in a desert – and that is exactly what it does. Like all flowering plants, the glasswort evolved as a freshwater species which tends to lose its sap through its roots when bathed in a high-density solution like sea water. So in the brackish or salty mud that surrounds it in estuaries, the plant must conserve its sap like a cactus rooted in an arid soil. Glasswort gained its common name from the old habit of burning the plants to obtain soda ash for use in glass-making. The stems are also edible and in the past they used to be a seasonal harvest. Today its value as a coloniser of bare mud far outweighs its taste, but its abilities are limited. The glasswort has short roots and so is easily dislodged from unstable mud and swept away by strong tidal currents. In such exposed places, only cord grasses stand any chance of becoming established.

Since 1870 the place of the glasswort as one of the principal pioneers of mud has been usurped by a brand new species of cord grass. This hybrid evolved naturally in Southampton waters when a native cord grass crossed with another from America. The result, known as Townsend's cord grass, has an extensive deep-growing root system and revealed itself as a more vigorous and effective binder of mud than either of its parents, a potential that did not go unnoticed. In 1935 around 1000 plants were successfully introduced to the Exe estuary, and these have now greatly extended and stabilised the salt marsh adjacent to the golf course at Dawlish Warren. The plants extend out into the shallows where they shelter a scavenging horde of young shore crabs, which scuttle amongst its shoots. At low tide the crabs bury themselves, leaving just a pair of eyes on stalks to peer above the surface.

On higher land, away from this flooded frontier, the ground is firmer and less salty. Here the success of the plants' silting power can be seen in a greater variety of growth and colour. Grey-green swathes of sea purslane are tinged yellow in summer by flowering spikes. Sea lavender blooms throughout the late summer months. Further up the estuary, bright clusters of sea aster buzz with insects that are attracted to the golden centre of its mauve-petalled flowers. Beyond, the salt marsh develops into a jungle, as a broad border of rushes gives way to dense stands of reed reaching high over the head. This is the summer haunt of reed warblers and, amongst the tangle of stems at the back of the bed, lies the delicately woven nest of a harvest mouse, the smallest rodent in Britain.

As spring progresses the birds that reside around the estuary begin to appear with their young. The grey herons are among the most conspicuous, because these big birds gather together in a nesting colony. One of the largest heronries in this part of England is situated in the nearby grounds of Powderham Castle. At the top of some of the tallest trees, untidy platforms of twigs are constructed,

Above: *The common snipe is normally a secretive and solitary bird hiding in the marsh, where it probes the mud for worms.* **Right:** *The curlew is the largest European shore bird.*

often built on the remnants of nests from the previous year. The nests have to be strong structures to support the weight of adults and young. A clutch of usually three to five light blue eggs is laid early, often in February, and incubated during some twenty-five days of sitting by both parents in turn. Aerial attack by marauding crows, partial to large eggs, requires a constant guard. The newly hatched young are almost comical looking, and require two months of frantic feeding before they are finally ready to fly from their lofty perch. During the summer herons wade the channels at low tide watching for flounders and other fish, or explore the adjacent streams and meadows for a surprisingly wide variety of prey, ranging from frogs to mice and water voles.

Nesting is a vulnerable time for birds, especially for the newly hatched that are accessible to predators on the ground, such as ducklings. Shelduck are the biggest and most boldly marked duck in Britain and, breaking with the tradition of drab females, both sexes are alike. However, this is not beneficial when breeding, and so the females retreat into nesting holes, which may be at the end of a 2-metre tunnel. Rabbit holes in sand dunes and hedgerows, or the shelter of boulders and bushes are all favoured sites. Even hollow trees are sometimes used by the duck to conceal her comfy nest of grass and feather down. The female incubates the eggs alone for about thirty days in the dim recess of her choosing, while the male remains on guard close by. Up to fourteen creamy white eggs eventually hatch into precocious balls of strikingly coloured fluff, dark brown above and white underneath. When dry, a few hours after hatching, the ducklings leave the nest and follow their parents in line. The nest may be over a kilometre from the estuary and the journey there on a warm morning in June can be eventful. As the waddling crocodile makes its way down to the relative safety of the tidal flats, it faces greater threats than cats, dogs, foxes, great black-backed gulls and other predators. Busy roads come close to the estuary, and the final hurdle is a railway track which runs along its edge. Once over this assault course barrier of stone and steel, the young can feed for the first time.

To begin with the family stays together, foraging for their diet of hydrobia snails and shrimps. The adults also search for small crabs and molluscs with their characteristic dabbling, swinging the head from side to side as they walk. When the feeding grounds are flooded they float and up-end to reach the bottom. The ducklings are unable to fly for at least nine weeks, but, unlike their parents, they can avoid attacks from the air by diving underwater. In July, when the young are only half grown, the majority of adult shelducks leave. The ducklings may then join together with other deserted families to form a crèche, assiduously watched over by a few remaining adults – the wildfowl equivalent of nannies. Almost the entire British population of adult shelducks head for the Heligoland Bight in the Baltic, off north-west Germany. There, more than 100 000 birds, including most of those from north-western Europe, gather in massive flocks to moult. A smaller number, some 1200–1500 shelduck, gather off Somerset, in Bridgwater Bay. Until recently their origin was unknown, but they are now thought to be mainly Irish birds.

In summer, there is a rise in human activity on the estuary. The daily flood brings a flurry of multi-coloured sailing craft and motor boats, making the most of deep-water channels. The turn of the tide goes almost unseen: one moment it is lapping at the salt marsh and the next draining from the flats. As the water recedes, mud banks begin to emerge and vast expanses, replenished by the tide, are revealed to the air. The multitudes that live in and on those surfaces stop feeding and take steps to protect themselves from being dried out. Lugworms and other mud dwellers simply withdraw into the waterlogged depths of their tubes. Hydrobia snails lie exposed in their millions, the fine shifting layer of mud in which they foraged having been carried away by the tide. Each tiny spire shell is closed by a disc fixed to the end of its foot, making a watertight seal. Similarly, cockles close their shells and mussels clamp shut.

The greatest danger these creatures face is not dehydration but flocks of hungry birds. The long-legged waders are specialist feeders, each in search of a particular prey. Their food is determined largely by the length and shape of their beak, but the actual diet can vary according to the abundance and size of their prey. Some birds even select their meals depending on the temperature, the redshank, for example, switching from sandhoppers to ragworms and burrowing bivalves, known as tellins, below 5°C. Birds that feed extensively on the same food do not necessarily have similar shaped beaks or build. Ringed plovers use their short sharp bills to extract individual hydrobia snails from their shells with a flick of the head, while the shelduck's broad red bill with a filter along the edge enables it to feast on thousands of the same little snails, shells and all. Curlews and godwits have the longest beaks, capable of reaching deep enough to drag lugworms from their burrows. Their probing is not entirely random. Since their lives depend on it, birds learn quickly where the most likely place for a meal may lie. In addition, beaks are highly sensitive to touch and birds such as the curlew have a prehensile tip which opens under the mud. Their ability to forage by feel alone means that these birds can hunt by day or night throughout the year, the hours of feeding governed solely by the rhythm of the tides.

Left: *Exmouth provides a fine view of wildfowl feeding on the most important eel grass bed in the estuary.*

Right: *Brent geese forage in the setting sun of late winter. Feeding time for most estuary birds is dictated by the tides rather than daylight.*

Oystercatchers are boldly marked birds, with black and white plumage, a bright orange bill, and a feeding method to match. Instead of employing the delicate and sensitive means by which other wading birds extract a meal, most oystercatchers use skill and brute force. The target prey depends upon the bird's age. Juvenile oystercatchers specialise in taking ragworms and peppery furrow shells, their tastes turning to larger shellfish as they grow older. A few adults seem to prefer cockles and periwinkles, but it is the vast banks of mussels which draw the biggest crowds. Cracking a mussel is an art learnt with age, and these birds employ two very distinct techniques for opening the shells – stabbing or hammering. Individual oystercatchers appear to use one method or the other, but not both.

While underwater, a mussel has its shells slightly apart to filter its plankton food. Stabbing oystercatchers take advantage of this by stalking shallow pools where mussels lie open to attack. The strike is swift but the ensuing thrusts must be powerful enough to cut the strong adductor muscle attempting to close the shells. Having dislodged and carried the hapless mussel ashore, a quick sideways movement of the bill levers the shells apart, forcing the mussel to reveal its flesh. In contrast the hammering oystercatchers ignore the underwater mussel, preferring to feed on the exposed beds where all the shells are tightly shut. They first tear a mussel off the bed and position it with the weaker underside of the shell uppermost. Then the bill is used like a pick-axe to bludgeon a hole large enough to insert the beak and sever the adductor muscle. The shell is finally levered apart, the flesh chiselled free in a single lump and swallowed. A skilled oystercatcher can open and clean out a mature mussel in under thirty seconds. This is an amazing feat as anyone who has ever attempted to open a mussel, even with a strong sharp knife, will appreciate.

The initial results of a major long-term study of oystercatchers has provided valuable insights into the feeding, behaviour and economic importance of these birds. They seem only to select the larger three-year-old mussels, and each bird can consume up to seventy-five a day. The level of predation is at its highest in winter, when the birds are thought to take 20–30 per cent of the mussels. Despite this, the impact of oystercatchers on the mussel population may be less than was previously thought. The number of mussels in a bed appears to be limited mainly by the availability of space for young spats to settle down.

Researchers have also studied the difference in feeding strategies among oystercatchers. They found that 'stabber' parents reared only stabbing young, and 'hammerer' parents reared only hammering young, which was not very surprising since behaviour in the bird world is usually instinctive. However, by swapping the eggs between a 'hammerer's' and a 'stabber's' nest, they discovered that the offspring followed their foster parents' example. This meant that, unusually in the bird world, oystercatchers can learn by watching. So an adult that discovers a new source of food or a new technique for obtaining it can pass that talent on to its chick. The evolutionary advantages of this go some way to explain the success of oystercatchers as a species.

Practice is needed to perfect the feeding techniques, and some youngsters have to wait for the chance because adults steal the biggest shells from them. A one-year-old bird can fend for itself but its efforts with mussels are slow and clumsy. Even older birds lose weight while rearing their young and only highly efficient feeders can rebuild that loss through the long winter months. As a result, oystercatchers do not begin breeding until four years of age. However, time is on their side because they are relatively long-lived birds, one ringed individual having reached twenty-nine years of age. Only a few oystercatchers breed in the south-west of Britain. The majority of the thousands of breeding adults and several hundred immatures that regularly winter on the Exe travel from Holland, northern Britain and even Norway. Along with many other migrants from the north, they begin to arrive in late summer.

On an August day the first sign of the tide's return is the movement of vessels moored nearest the mouth, slowly falling back into line. In silence and increasing speed, the water creeps back. It seeks out the lowest levels, progressively drowning the rippled, current-carved depressions in sand and mud. The sheet of ruffled water brings relief to the hordes of shrimps, worms and shellfish under siege from warm dry winds and ravenous birds. In the returning flow laden with new supplies of food, crabs emerge to forage, shells open and siphons push up like periscopes. As the estuary begins to flood, the boats tug hard on their lines. Cormorants, carried upstream, fish the incoming currents, while on the banks, herons keep pace with the rising level. The deeper channels between the mudbanks soon brim and spill out over the flats. Along the advancing front, a walking and flying throng feasts on the returning tide. They provide a colourful spectacle because most of the birds still retain much of their bright, summer, breeding plumage.

Black-headed gulls in raucous mob fill the air with their incessant squawking. Godwits, both black-tailed and bar-tailed, still resplendent in their chestnut breeding livery, wade in the shallows probing for worms. These elegant long-billed birds take advantage of the larger lugworms' need every 45 minutes to push up towards the surface, in order to eject their cast of waste sand. The bar-tailed godwits have flown the furthest to reach the estuary, breeding in northern Europe and arctic Russia. While the main breeding ground of the black-tailed is Iceland, a few now nest in Britain. They were once resident in some numbers but were driven out in the nineteenth century by being hunted for food and the draining of the fens in East Anglia. Only since 1952 have they again become a British breeding bird. The long curved bills of wintering curlew and its migrant cousin, the wimbrel, mingle among the flocks along with several redshank and dunlin. In a separate party, some arctic-breeding grey plovers keep pace with the tide. All the birds feed frantically, moving quickly over the mud that remains.

As the tide rises higher and higher, the flocks are pushed further up the flats. In the more remote parts of the estuary, sheltered by cord grass and rushes, the feeding flocks come to a halt. The flats disappear from view beneath the rippling tide and the birds rest at high water. After preening and sorting loose feathers, many of the birds tuck their beaks over their backs and raise a leg. Standing on one leg is common among waders and, although the reason is not entirely clear, it undoubtedly adds to their comfort and warmth. Indeed, so reluctant are some to put down a dried foot that, if forced to move by a final surge of wavelets, they will hop to higher ground.

An undisturbed, high-tide roost is of prime importance because, when unable to feed, the birds need to rest. The largest and most permanent high-water roost is located in the lee of Dawlish Warren. Purpose built by the Devon Wildlife Trust with advice from the Royal Society for the Protection of Birds (RSPB), this avian leisure island is successfully managed by Teignbridge Council, which also funds the reserve wardens here. Overlooked by a hide, it has become a mecca for ardent birdwatchers and casual walkers, providing local residents and holidaymakers with a superb sheltered view without disturbing the birds.

A sunny August bank holiday brings people flocking to the beach on the seaside of the warren. Just a few hundred metres away, migrant birds are also arriving for a stay at the roost. Observed through a pair of binoculars, the site seems at times akin to the bird world equivalent of an international airport. The daily arrivals and departures vary with the seasons but August is one of the peak times. The large numbers of godwits alone make this a site of international importance. A few ruff and reeves are also seen each year, although the females may easily be confused at a distance with the occasional greenshank. Most other species of wading birds found in Britain also appear at this roost at one time or another, including little stint, curlew sandpiper, sanderling and knot.

The annual influx of terns is a particularly noisy and exciting time. Apart from the occasional roseate, and 100 or more common terns, the biggest numbers are made up by screeching flocks of sandwich terns. Named after the seaside town in Kent, they sadly no longer breed there, but do successfully nest in over forty colonies from Shetland to the south coast of England. At the end of summer over 600 of these attractive birds can usually be counted on this estuary. The

Above: *A high tide roost in one of the quieter parts of the estuary allows godwits, grey plovers and other small waders to rest between feeds.*

Left: *The European spoonbill seen here on the Exe, is almost becoming an annual visitor to estuaries in the south-west of England.*

Right: *The avocet is the most famous of all the winter visiting birds on the Exe Estuary, easily recognised by its upturned bill and striking plumage.*

Exe is a seasonal stopover on their journey south to wintering grounds off the coast of west Africa.

Oystercatchers arrive at the roost in spectacularly noisy fashion, appearing as a huge piping flock of black and white wings. During September their numbers can increase to over 4000 birds, a truly impressive sight. On landing they space out evenly, a beak's reach apart, and monopolise the highest point. At its fringes ringed plovers take a brief rest from their busy lives, while the turnstones continue to feed in the manner that befits their name. The main turnstone roost lies further up the estuary, where they crowd together on top of a brickbuilt breakwater at Starcross.

On a September day, the tide was approaching its full height and the warren roost was packed with birds, when a streaming tight-knit flock of more small birds came across the water, flying low. They flashed white undersides as they banked away, and all but disappeared when dark backs were turned. These were dunlin, among the smallest wading birds, whose great flocks perform the most incredible aerobatics. They climb and dive in a fluid string, massing and then spilling out of the air in a shower of falling wings to land near the water's edge. A few may well have nested in Britain, but the vast majority would have flown in from their breeding grounds in the far north around arctic shores. Their numbers build up on the Exe over autumn until by mid-winter some 6000 dunlin are regularly using the roost.

Like the peregrines which prey on the dunlin, many of the birds that come to plunder the spoils of rich estuarine mud are predictable visitors, often arriving within a few days of their appearance in previous years. Others are less frequent, some rare, and a few are real surprises. In recent years pure white little egrets have been seen wading in the shallows in late summer, energetically whirling, stabbing and dashing around in circles as they prey on small crabs and fish. These handsome birds seem to be expanding from their more usual southern range. Another equally exotic visitor, the spoonbill, puts in an appearance almost annually on many of the sheltered creeks and estuaries in the south-west. Spoonbills bred in Britain were found in both Sussex and Middlesex in the 1500s were still nesting in East Anglia in the following century. Today the nearest breeding colonies of these extraordinary birds are in Holland and France. The spoon-shaped bill, which gave rise to its name, serves a practical purpose as this odd-looking bird wades through the water, swinging its head from side to side to sift the surface mud for small fish, snails and plants.

The first of the autumn gales brings down silt-laden floods and whips the water into a muddy cauldron. Lapwing and curlew make use of nearby fields.

per3

233

Snipe need cover and so are seldom found in the open, preferring to probe the marshes and soggy meadows. In the shelter of the salt marsh and other lee shores, increasing numbers of wildfowl gather, for the Exe is internationally important for them too. Wigeon overwinter in considerable numbers, at times up to 5000 birds, along with several hundred teal and mallard. For the increasing number of people that come to watch the birds, small flocks of pintails, especially the handsome drakes, are an annual attraction. The past few years have also seen a newcomer to these shores. The long-tailed duck, which is an arctic breeder at the extreme south-west of its wintering range. More commonly, a rising tide finds diving ducks, frequenting the channels, including usually a pair of goldeneye and parties of red-breasted merganser.

One of the highlights of the year is the arrival in November of the first big flocks of brent geese from the north. The dark-breasted race of the brent breeds in the Russian arctic and spends the winter months along the milder coastline of the English Channel. Another race of the same goose, the pale-breasted, breeds in Greenland and Spitsbergen, and winters mainly in Ireland, with only a few individuals reaching the south coast. Brent geese are fast-flying birds, and head south in loose but well co-ordinated flocks. They arrive on a brisk northerly wind, winging in low over the water. By late afternoon thousands of brent geese may have gathered on the rising tide, and as darkness descends more birds may fly in, the size of the flock growing as the weeks go by.

A fine winter dawn provides a picturesque scene, with weak sun illuminating a flat calm sea and some 3500 brent geese floating close inshore. Drifting among the massive flock are thousands of small wildfowl. At peak times the Exe estuary alone supports some 7000 wildfowl and nearly 15000 wading birds. Sound carries far on such a morning and the still, crisp air is filled with amazing noise. Geese grunt and call to each other in a constant clamour, while the whistling note of wigeon adds to the estuarine chorus. In early winter the geese remain in family parties, consisting of parents and between three and five young. Juveniles have pale parallel lines on their wing coverts, and lack the distinctive white neck mark of the adults. They tend to keep clear of their more dominant peers until the tide begins to drop, when the birds have other matters in mind – food. Tails point skyward revealing their bright white underparts as they up-end in the shallows over the lush, eel grass beds. Long necks enable the geese to reach the plants before the other wildfowl, giving them longer to satisfy their hunger. Only mute swans have a head start on brent geese. Although seldom present in large numbers, over 100 swans have been counted at times.

The brent geese continue feeding on the estuary for as long as possible. As

Brent geese flock to low lying meadows in late winter when food supplies in the estuary begin to get low.

the winter progresses, the remaining eel grass gradually disappears, stripped and torn by hundreds of hungry beaks or ravaged by winter storms. The beds nearest to the shore, and possible danger, are the last to be consumed. At low tide, when the water has drained from the feeding ground, the flats are accessible from the land, and the big concentrations of wildfowl attract large numbers of people to the shore. Most are eager to watch from a distance, but a few are not so thoughtful. While people approaching too close may simply cause the geese to move away from the last supplies of food, their dogs running loose panic the birds into flight. High tide brings different dangers to the birds. The most sensitive areas for feeding birds are marked with bright yellow buoys, which keep power boats and water skiers away from them. However, windsurfers present a greater problem as many frequent the shallows, especially novices. Responsible members of the local clubs try to keep clear of the large flocks of wildfowl, particularly the geese, but others appear not to care. In recent years a new peace-shattering threat has emerged in the shape of the furiously speeding marine equivalent of the motor bike.

In these and other ways, the enjoyment of many people is being ruined by a few individuals, who are also putting thousands of birds' lives at risk. Disturbance kills, although death is seldom instantaneous and the bodies may never be found. Weakened birds may succumb to the waves out in the middle of the estuary, or a thousand miles away en route to their breeding grounds. The effects may be even more insidious. If the birds are not in peak condition, they can fail to nest or lose their chicks to one of nature's many thieves. Even healthy birds may not succeed, as a Dutch research team of a German expedition reported in 1989. The arctic spring in that year was some three weeks late, and even by the end of July they found that the coastal sea was still completely ice-covered. This provided an easy access for ground predators to pillage the birds' breeding islands. The researchers saw no young among the 45 000 brent geese moulting in the area that year. The effects of increasing disturbance on British estuaries, added to the vagaries of nature, may not be apparent the following season, but the number of birds returning each winter could slowly decline.

When the geese first arrive at the estuary, their urgent need is to replenish the reserves lost on their long migration flight south. Supplies are limited and they rush to graze, not through gluttony but the simple need to survive. They require regular sources of nourishment during winter and disturbance means they must consume even more. The few hours at high tide allow the brent geese time to rest, preen and ready themselves for more feeding. As spring approaches the birds leave the depleted beds of eel grass to feed in the surrounding meadows. No longer protected by open views across mud and water, the birds are wary and feeding often appears frantic. The purchase of an important flood meadow site by the RSPB has given the geese a secure source of grass, and people a convenient focal point to watch the wintering wildfowl.

There is one bird that people are prepared to travel hundreds of miles just to catch a glimpse of – the avocet. A strikingly attractive plumage and the elegance of a graceful upturned bill are the distinctive lines of this long-legged bird. In early winter, the first flock settles on the estuary mud, its contrasting black and white markings brightening the dullest day. Even the avocet's movement, a stately walk and scything motion of its bill, puts it into a class of its own. The real finesse of their feeding technique is only apparent at close quarters. They seek out the dense shoals of opossum shrimps on mud banks and along the edge of the channels. Then singly or in a group, they advance delicately on their long blue-grey legs, skimming the surface from side to side as they feel for the slightest movement. Sweeping and swallowing, they stand where the shrimps are plentiful or wade slowly but surely across the flats. Although the slim upturned bill is unsuitable for deep probing, the birds pick off any small crustaceans or ragworms that venture close to the surface. After the turn of the tide they continue to feed as the waters rise, first wading, then swimming and up-ending. When finally out of their depth, they paddle in a tight flotilla until their muddy dining table is again exposed.

The return of the avocet to Britain is an outstanding achievement of bird protection. In the 1700s, they were plentiful, breeding in the fens of eastern England. Then drainage reduced their numbers and the birds were shot for their feathers and their eggs stolen to add to the ingredients of puddings. The last nesting colony of avocets survived in Norfolk until around 1825 when that too was finally destroyed. In the years following the Second World War, a few pairs, perhaps displaced by wartime flooding in Holland, began to nest on Minsmere and Havergate Island in Suffolk. The sites were purchased and secured by the RSPB, whose subsequent management has enabled a thriving population to develop. Over 250 pairs now nest at a dozen different locations, and British-born avocets are regular winter visitors to Devon in flocks over 300 strong.

The breathtaking appearance of the avocets, the huge flocks of geese and the haunting cry of the curlew linger in the memories of visitors to the estuary. For many, these and other birds are the life of the tidal flats. But the real strength of the estuary grows from its mud and wriggles through its sand, an incredible teeming world of weird worms, fascinating shells and extraordinary plants, all fed by an unending supply of nutrients from both the land and the sea.

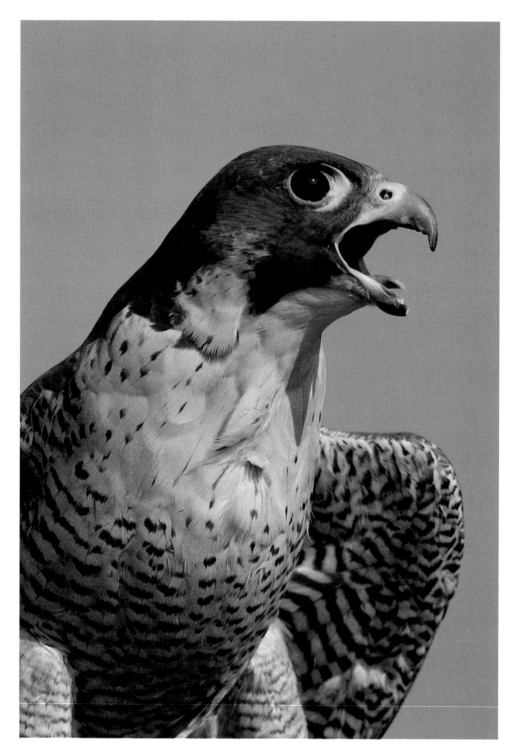

The peregrine is the most spectacular bird of the sea cliff, renowned for its high speed flight. They mate for life, often returning year after year to the same nest site.

CHAPTER FOUR

Life on the Edge

*T*HE HISTORY OF the earth's formation is held within its rocks, and there are few places where these can be read more clearly than in the sheer towering face of a sea cliff. Here, the rocks' origins, whether from the furnaces of volcanic activity, ancient reefs and showers of lime-rich shells, or the deposits of flooding many millennia ago, lie exposed and are gradually being worn away. Carved by the destructive energy of wind and wave, the cliff has other elements at work on its ramparts too. Though more subtle, they have the power to move mountains, albeit a bit at a time.

During the course of their making and the subsequent pressures and strains, most rocks acquire lines of weakness, fractures and faults. These may lie hidden for millions of years, but eventually the scars surface. Winter rain seeps into the freshly exposed cracks and overnight temperatures plunge. The water begins to freeze and as it does so, it expands. The mechanical force shatters the surface layers, prising off flakes and small chunks that remain held in an icy grasp. Frost seldom lasts long on these coasts, and as the ice gradually melts in the morning sun, the day is greeted by a tumbling salvo of fragments. Within the rock the effect of frost is less evident, but potentially far more destructive. The relentless cycle of freezing and thawing, expansion and contraction repeated year after year, turns hairline fractures into yawning fissures that extend deeper and deeper inside. If they meet bigger breaks, the cracks really begin to show. The cliff face becomes unstable and finally huge sections crash to the shore below. The processes of weathering and coastal erosion dismantle hard rock only gradually, but in softer material their effects can be more dramatic.

This was seen on Christmas night in 1839 by people at Bindon near Axmouth on the east Devon cliffs, not far from the Dorset border. The coastguards on duty that evening heard terrible sounds in the darkness, 'resembling the rending of cloth'. The ground shook, great cracks opened beneath their feet, and off Culverhole Point they saw a great shape rise from the sea. The earth movements were not seismic tremors but shock waves from a collapse precipitated by an unusually wet autumn and unfestive heavy rain that preceded Christmas. Later it was found that a huge landslip of some eight million tonnes had carried away a massive slice of the cliffland countryside below Bindon Moor and Dowlands Farm. Six hectares of farmland, complete with hedgerows, trees and sown wheatfield, had slipped down towards the sea and was marooned by a gaping ravine nearly 1 kilometre in length and up to 130 metres deep. The subsidence had thrown up a new reef just offshore, but this was soon destroyed by wave action.

The following February saw the beginning of more earth movements as a further series of smaller slips extended the collapse towards Whitlands and Charton Bay. But it was the first and biggest 'earthquake' at Bindon that drew the crowds, marvelling at the scale of the disaster and the wheat that continued to grow and ripen in its novel location. The site became a public curiosity and on 25 August 1840 a party of smartly dressed reapers and accompanying maidens, armed with golden sickles tied with blue ribbons, crossed the newly named Great Chasm to the stranded section of cliff called Goat Island. There, according to a local newspaper of the time, they were accompanied with great ceremony by a band and watched by more than 6000 spectators.

Today the 7 kilometres or so of coastline between Axmouth and Lyme Regis are rugged and dangerous, still prone to subsidence. It is known as the Undercliff. Here the largest naturally regenerated ash forest in Britain dominates the dense, virtually impenetrable undergrowth, concealing deep crevices, boggy ground and dark green pools. For some people the Undercliff is a nightmarish place, where unwary walkers are lured at their peril from the well-worn path into the clutching barbs of brambles reaching out from dim labyrinths of twisted roots and fallen trunks. Every year the rescue services are called out to find people who have become lost or injured after straying from the one tortuous trail. For others, though, it is a wild yet peaceful retreat, offering hidden treasures, one of the few places in Britain where nature appears completely untamed. A clue to its natural importance can be gained from the fact that it was designated a National Nature Reserve in 1955. Covering nearly 325 hectares, the Undercliff is carefully maintained by English Nature, which endeavours to preserve its wealth of wild features despite the fact that large parts are occasionally on the move.

The subsidence is usually gradual, measurable in months rather than minutes, which is why the cataclysmic slump in Victorian times became an historical event. But large-scale landslips do still occur. The winter of 1986–87 saw the

Above: *Thick growth dominates the Undercliff. Its trees are tangled with honeysuckle and traveller's joy.*
Below: *The tranquil beauty of the Undercliff and Charton Bay belies the unstable dangerous terrain.*

start of another collapse on National Trust property just east of Lyme Regis. Again the powerful forces of erosion were at work, this time turning a peaceful farm meadow into a demolition site in just a few weeks. The precise causes of slips may be complex but the basic agent of destruction in each case is water. The underlying strata are composed of ancient chalk, sandstone and a form of crumbling slate, a type of shale. Many of the layers of rock were laid down during the age of the dinosaurs. Some, such as the Jurassic Lias Clay and the Cretaceous Gault, are impermeable to water, while others, such as the overlying Cretaceous Upper Greensand, dissolve when wet. The result of heavy rain on the strata is akin to drenching a precariously balanced pile of bricks some of which are made of soluble material. The waterlogged shale slides over the slippery clay, and this occasionally leads to a landslide.

But such instability brings its own benefits. Today, even the most dogged developer or enthusiastic farmer would not seriously contemplate disturbing the land. On a calm summer's day, a sparkling azure sea and segments of white cliff, jutting from a lush blanket of green, provide a scene so unspoiled as to be scarcely credible. Two hundred years ago this coastline was very different and probably far from wild. Sheep roamed and grazed its rough pasture, no doubt vastly outnumbered by a thriving population of rabbits, which had yet to be decimated by the highly contagious disease of myxomatosis. The turf, especially at the eastern end, was more like a park, a place for picnicking and games of cricket. Now woodland effectively cloaks this part of the coast, and the Undercliff has an exotic feel. Protected from cold northerly winds, and with a sunshine record well above average, it is warm. It is also wet, for it is endowed with an ample supply of water and even in the driest weather, when inland areas are parched, sea mist rolling inshore drenches the woodland foliage. In the few clearings that afford any view, ash trees rise high above the dense undergrowth, choked by rampant ivy and draped in wild clematis. Their liana-like stems, hanging from the branches, reinforce the impression that this is some subtropical rainforest rather than an English shore.

Primroses flower early in spring in the Undercliff, hurrying to bloom before the summer canopy of leaves brings gloom to the chasm. The place is a botanist's dream with a rich variety of plants, including eleven different species of orchid. One of the earliest to flower grows in the grasslands of an isolated plateau, rising from the surrounding forest. The green-winged orchid survives, as do most of the other chalk-meadow plants here, only through the strenuous efforts of the reserve warden and helpers. Scrub continually threatens to engulf Goat Island and annual clearances are necessary. One of the real treasures of this island, and elsewhere in the reserve, is the descriptively named bee orchid. Its flowers, which mimic its namesake, are beautifully adapted for cross-pollination by bees. Orchids flower in succession, the oldest low down on the spike and the youngest at the top. They are amazingly slow to mature, sometimes taking several years to develop from a tiny wind-blown seed. In terms of size and variety of colour and form, orchids are the most diverse family of flowers in the world. Sadly, some of them also rank among the rarest plants on earth. Even in the Undercliff they are not common, but spectacular spikes of marsh, greater butterfly, early purple, pyramidal and fragrant orchids, and marsh helleborine and common twayblade, have all been recorded within the reserve. Less spectacular and surely among the strangest of all is the usually solitary bird's nest orchid.

This plant flourishes beneath high-rise trees and larger shrubs, where others struggle to survive. Green plants contain the green pigment, chlorophyll, which enables them to manufacture essential food using the energy in sunlight, and they cannot thrive in the twilight zone of dense shade. The bird's nest orchid, however, has no chlorophyll and is devoid of leaves. Rising from its tight-knit root mass, which gives rise to its name, is just a scaly spike bearing yellow-brown flowers. The orchid draws its nourishment mainly from the deep layers of dead and decaying vegetation that litter the woodland floor. Its fungus-infected root ball supplies the remaining nutrients that cannot be extracted from rotting vegetation. Indeed, the bird's nest orchid is so well adapted to life in the dark that it has even been found to flower occasionally underground.

Butterflies and moths, beetles and a multitude of flies forage among the luxuriant growth. But not all species of these insects need to find food when adult. There is one beetle that is thought to eat only during its larval stage. The young glow-worm dispatches snails, overtaking its lumbering prey and spearing the mollusc with its tubular jaws. The hapless snail is injected with a dark fluid which first paralyses and then reduces the victim to a juice. Drinking from the shell, the larva sucks up its meal. Glow-worms were far more common in Victorian times than now, when urban sprawl, land drainage and the widespread use of insecticides have all taken their toll. There is another form of pollution too that has an incalculable effect on the glow-worm population. A mature male glow-worm flies to find a flightless female, guided by the cold chemical light she emits from the tail-end segments of her egg-bloated body. The male is particularly sensitive to the narrow spectrum of light produced by the female, but is easily diverted by a brighter source. For glow-worms, street and house lights are pollutants, spoiling the darkness and their chances of finding a mate. In the intense black nights of the Undercliff, there are no such

Above: *The bee orchid is a flower of the cliff grasslands, named after the insect it imitates and attracts for pollination.*

Left: *The Axemouth–Lyme Undercliff is a remarkable nature reserve. Huge sections of the collapsed cliff remain isolated by deep tree-filled chasms.*

distractions and glow-worms continue to thrive on the slopes.

Darkness also brings out the bats, which fly squeaking overhead. Britain's largest, the noctule, has a wingspan of up to 39 centimetres, about the width of this book when open, and is primarily a woodland species. Other bats found there include the long-eared and lesser horseshoe, which inhabit tree holes and caves in the cliffs. Last but not least, the tiny pipistrelle is common almost everywhere and also roosts in the confines of cracks in tree trunks and rock faces. At dusk and in the growing light of dawn, the flitting high-speed manoeuvres of the bats can be seen as they take and eat insects on the wing. We can only marvel at their aerial prowess in a world sensed solely through the echoes of the high-pitched sounds they produce.

In contrast, the mainly nocturnal badgers sense their environment principally by smell, above and below ground. Although badgers are found throughout the country, those on the cliff tops and below are on the very edge of their range. They are sociable animals, and occupy territories in closely related groups. Ownership of a territory is marked by a series of latrines strategically sited along the borders. Members of a group smear odour on each other from special glands located under the tail, giving individuals a smelly family identity. Their home is a complex of tunnels and chambers dug with powerful paws. This sett is typically 10–20 metres in length, but some extend up to 100 metres into hillsides on easily excavated ground. Badgers are creatures of habit and regularly used tracks fan out from the home sett, linking foraging grounds with other setts and territorial frontiers.

Badgers are considered by many to be the ultimate omnivores, their daily diet depending on the food available. Rabbits, rats, mice, moles and even hedgehogs are tackled, along with frogs, slugs and snails. Beetles and grubs of both bees and wasps are sought after, and sometimes make up a good part of their meals. They very rarely kill lambs, but still-born lambs are occasionally taken. In winter, carrion becomes especially important, while summer brings a different bounty. Windfall apples, pears, plums, acorns, hazelnuts, wild strawberries and blackberries are all gobbled with relish. When times get really hard, badgers will even eat grass and clover, and in some areas they are particularly partial to corn, oats and wheat. However, the single most important item on their extensive menu is the earthworm. In the west country, it was discovered that three-quarters of the badgers investigated had recently dined on earthworms, and of those nearly two-thirds had consumed nothing else.

If you walk along the main path that winds its way through the Undercliff, you will see various side tracks from time to time. These you take at your peril, not only because the rules of the reserve restrict access to the main path. The tracks inevitably pass under a low fallen log or into a dense thorn thicket, and only then will it dawn on you that you have been following a badger's trail and can progress no further. Deer are not so constrained. They move freely and in silence, melting into seemingly impenetrable scrub. The Undercliff supports a large population of roe deer, as can be seen from the frequency of their hoof slots found crossing and following the main path.

The sure-footed roe deer roam the broken cliffscape with ease. They are surprisingly small creatures, which appear almost tailless. A big black nose and white chin mark are distinctive, but the usual sight in these woods is a bounding rear end as a deer vanishes into the scrub. The only consolation is that the view does allow you to tell the sexes apart. In summer, the doe has a bright white rump patch and that of the buck is more buff coloured and less conspicuous. In winter, the rump patches are equally distinct in both sexes, but are kidney-shaped in the male and an inverted heart shape in the female. The reddish-brown coat also becomes thicker, darker and greyer.

The sexes usually live apart but come together to mate in midsummer. It is during their rut, which lasts from mid-July to the middle of August, that the bucks are at their most aggressive. Unusually among deer, many roe bucks hold a territory for most of the year, not just during the rut, and scent plays an important part in this. Although deer have excellent sight and incredibly acute hearing, smell comes into its own in the confines of a wood. The bucks use scent glands on their hind legs and between the antlers to smear their signs of ownership on trunks and leaves. These form relatively long-lasting and highly effective noticeboards. At dusk the deer leave their daytime retreats and emerge hesitantly from the woods to spend the hours of darkness grazing on the clifftop meadows and grassy islands.

The Undercliff's dense undergrowth, variety of habitat and rich supply of wild fruits and nuts help sustain many smaller mammals. Wood mice and bank voles are common, and the abundance of honeysuckle and hazel allow the dormouse to thrive. It is a nocturnal creature and hibernates throughout the winter. Smaller still, and an insectivore rather than a rodent, is the tiny pygmy shrew. This active little predator feeds on beetles and spiders with a particular predilection for woodlice. Close to the minimum size at which a mammal can maintain its body heat, the pygmy shrew survives only by a hectic cycle of feeding and resting every three hours or less, throughout the day and night. All these small creatures are, in turn, preyed upon by weasels and tawny owls.

Even the healthiest wild animals carry passengers from time to time, an

Right: *Roe deer are common in the tangled jungle of the Undercliff. Shy and wary animals they normally emerge from the undergrowth to graze from dusk to dawn.*

Below: *The crumbling cliffs of Lyme Regis are famed for their ancient fossil-bearing rocks.*

unwelcome horde of parasites. Ticks are especially common in summer in the Undercliff. These distant relatives of the spider have eight short, stubby legs and powerful jaws, and spend much of their time on a leaf or stem, waiting for a passing meal. Special organs on the ends of their front legs, highly sensitive to changes in odour and humidity, detect the looming presence of warm-blooded hosts. Even on regularly used tracks, a fox, deer or bare-legged walker may seldom come quite close enough. However, time is on the tick's side because it can survive several years between bites. When an animal does brush past, the tick clings to the hair of the host and then fights down through the fur coat to the skin. There, it holds on with its teeth and, inserting its barbed snout, begins to suck the nourishing blood. After gorging itself for several hours, the tick has swollen from a flattened creature a few millimetres in length to one the size of a large pea. The bloated tick drops off and, if mature enough, it will then breed. For people at least, ticks are generally more of a pest than a peril, but warnings are increasingly being given about the potentially serious Lyme's disease, which can be transmitted by ticks to humans.

The difficult terrain of the Undercliff is no hindrance to ticks, nor to the migrant birds that are attracted to its sheltered woods in the spring. By early May the Great Chasm and deep ravines are alive with warblers, including the chiffchaff and willow warbler. These birds are so similar in appearance they almost defy recognition until they open their beaks, when the monotonously repeated 'chiff-chaff' song of one can be distinguished from the descending warble of the other. In recent years the winters there have been so warm that many chiffchaffs no longer migrate. Blackcaps also arrive from Scandinavia to remain throughout the coldest months. But one bird that does head south each autumn returns from Africa in the spring to give a performance that is quite outstanding, even by warbler standards. In the gathering dusk, the nightingale's melodious song is amplified by a natural amphitheatre, the surrounding cliffs.

Wind prevails on a cliff. Even on the stillest of days, cool air above the sea is drawn to the shore by the rising warmth of the land, and the updrafts produced are exploited by the bigger birds. Gulls travel many miles without a single flap, and the developing thermals provide all the lift a buzzard needs to soar and explore. As it circles overhead with wing-tips splayed, the buzzard's plaintive call echoes from the steep white walls. Gulls and crows may occasionally mob these broad-winged birds of prey. However, a buzzard can easily outdistance most pursuers with a lazy flap or two, and is quite capable of defending itself against a more determined attack. It simply flips over on to its back and meets the aggressor with its talons. When hunting, the buzzard's leisurely flight is far from an aimless wander. The bird quarters the ground, its remarkable sight being capable of detecting the tiniest movement. Although rabbits and other small mammals are the most sought-after prey, it will sometimes feed on other birds, and more often on lizards, earthworms and beetles. It is also not averse to taking carrion.

Common in hill country with abundant food, buzzards are a familiar sight in the west country, and the Undercliff has a resident pair nesting on a ledge. The buzzards' nest is a bulky platform of sticks, often decorated with leaves or the fronds of seaweed. Both parents build it and share the duty of incubating two or three white eggs, often marked in chocolate or reddish brown. If kept warm and dry, and turned at regular intervals, the eggs hatch in around thirty-six days. Young buzzards grow fat on the household diet of rabbit when such food is plentiful. The breeding success of the buzzard was badly hit in 1953 when myxomatosis devastated the population of its favourite meal, but since then its numbers have soared. After forty-five days in the nest the fledglings are capable of flight. Their first efforts are not the unhurried wing beat of the adults, but a more undignified scramble into the nearest tree. Practice makes perfect, and in the following days they fly back and forth along the cliff, learning the aerial skills that will set them up for life. Within a week they begin to follow their parents, taking to the air in a mewing band that rides the gentle sea breezes.

If you take a bird's-eye view of the coastline around Lyme Regis, the extent and precarious nature of these crumbling cliffs becomes apparent. In places the faces are so frequently weathered by rainfall and wind that even the most vigorous plants cannot take root. Those that do manage to gain a hold on the brink are likely to be lost over the edge in a cliff fall that may yield more unexpected finds. In 1809 Mary Anning, a local girl then just twelve years of age, found and excavated the fossil remains of a giant fish-like reptile. It was the almost complete skeleton of a 180-million-year-old icthyosaur, 8 metres in length. One of the first of its kind known to science, the fossil now resides in the Natural History Museum in London.

Since then, the crumbling cliffs of Lyme Regis have become a happy hunting ground for fossil collectors. Reptile remains are only rarely found, but the fossil shells of archaic marine molluscs, such as ammonites, are relatively common. In some areas, ammonite shells lie so thickly they form solid bands embedded in the soft blue rock. Some shells are the width of a small coin while those of other species may be the size of an articulated truck tyre. When alive, the ammonites were not sluggish snails trailing heavily across ancient seabeds. Their coiled

Above: *The importance of Berry Head as a nature reserve, lies not only in the fact that it is the largest outcrop of Devonian limestone in Britain, but also because of its magnificent plant and bird life.*

Right: *The cirl bunting is one of the rarest breeding birds in Britain mainly confined to the coastal strip of South Devon. It is primarily a Mediterranean species.*

Far right: *Berry Head holds the largest colony of auks on the south coast. Throughout the summer the cliff ledges (opposite) echo to the calls of guillemots, razorbills and other seabirds such as fulmars and kittiwakes.*

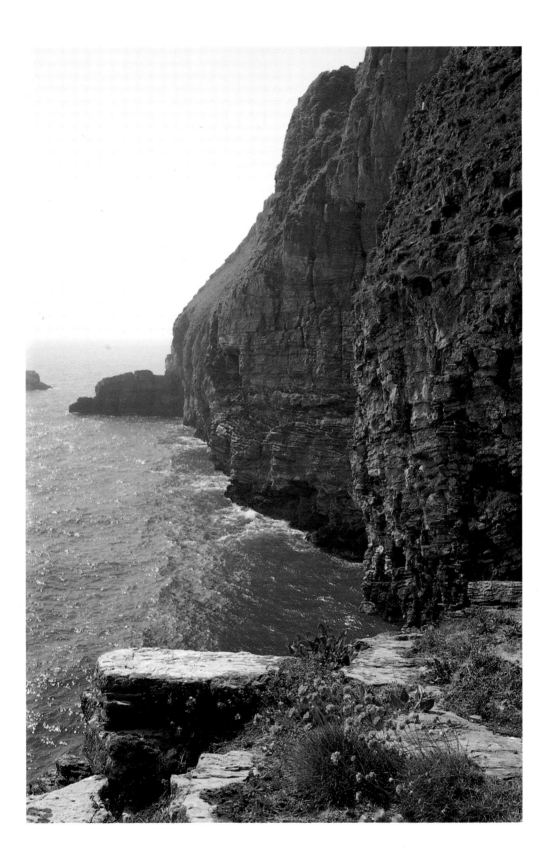

shells contained a series of curving walls, which formed effective flotation chambers. Even giants of their kind were buoyant, weightless in water, and cruised with ease through the depths of prehistoric seas.

Erosion occurs along the whole south coast of Britain, from the white chalk cliffs of Dover to the granite at Land's End, and its results are often spectacular, sometimes incredible and occasionally bizarre. The bedding planes between layers of rock are widened by the regular pulse and power of the sea. Different rocks, which look almost identical, may erode at slightly different rates, forming stacks and arches, gullies, blow holes, ledges and sheltered inlets. To the west of Lyme Regis and the Undercliff lie old red sandstone cliffs that have been sculpted in extraordinary ways, resembling the crazy carvings of some monstrous wood-boring worm. The intricate pattern of hollows and holes is the product of thousands of years of etching by the action of wind and water.

Such soft stone is easy to excavate but only creatures with the power of flight can reach its steep faces. They include seabirds and, in the most sheltered parts of the sea cliff, a colony of sand martins takes advantage of the softest layers. Their tiny feet scratch away at the sandstone to dig a tunnel up to a metre long. Elsewhere, the closely related house martin occasionally returns to its ancestral home. Before there were buildings with eaves, these birds nested on cliffs and cave walls. Feeding almost entirely on the wing, they seldom visit the ground except to collect mud for nest-building. Pairs of house martins breed in loose colonies and each pair constructs its nest from little beak-sized balls of mud mixed with saliva, grass and roots.

Sheltered parts of the coast often have higher winter temperatures than inland and so can offer year-round pickings for birds dependent on insects and seeds. The gentle slopes above many cliffs provide opportunities for such birds to nest near the sea. Stonechats nest extensively among the gorse, which in places forms dense scrub; and, in just a few locations, one of the rarest breeding birds in Britain makes its home. The entire British breeding population of the cirl bunting is thought to number not more than 140 pairs of birds and the bulk of those are confined to a narrow coastal strip in south Devon. This Mediterranean species is at the extreme northern edge of its range in Britain and seems to survive best in the mild south-west adjacent to farmland, where stubble fields offer annual gluts of grain.

As it calls from a tree, the male cirl bunting's attractive brown and yellow markings are some compensation for its brief trill of a song. The nest is an untidy woven bundle of grass and roots built on a foundation of moss and hidden in a hedgerow or bush. The adults return frequently to feed their growing brood of up to four young. Little is known about this bird's habits, partly because of its rarity and also because its shy, almost secretive lifestyle makes it difficult to watch. In one pair that was observed, the parents often appeared together at the nest or arrived within a short time of each other. Although the male is not thought to help much with rearing the young, this particular male would often perch on a bush top several metres away, checking if the coast was clear. He would then drop down into cover and make his way through the hedge. The chicks, responding to his faint contact call, would rise as one from the bowels of the nest, beaks agape, clamouring for a meal. The female delivered food in a similar way and would often wait as he did for the delivery of a white faecal sac from one of their young. She would pick it up carefully and then fly, keeping low to the ground, until she was some distance away and drop it. This behaviour is followed by most birds of her size, because white splashes around the nest would act as a beacon for predators.

Small birds face many hazards nesting around sea cliffs, not least the raucous colonies of scavenging gulls. The large, bold but wary herring gulls are found in great numbers, their head-thrown cry being the familiar call of the seaside. They eat almost anything, from crab and fish offal to young birds, including their own kind. In the noisy activity of their breeding colonies, parent birds must guard their nest against other marauding gulls, from the day the eggs are laid. Three is the usual clutch and they are incubated for about twenty-six days. The most dangerous time comes when both parent birds must leave to find food in order to satisfy the chicks' growing demands. Young herring gulls leave the nest after a week or so but seldom travel far, remaining hidden close by. Their speckled down and developing feathers merge with the cliff and, unless they draw attention to themselves, they are likely to fledge successfully. However, it will be another four years before they are fully mature and can begin breeding themselves.

Seabirds are attracted to steep cliffs by the powerful updrafts that buffet them, but the birds do have other requirements. They need plenty of ledges that provide firm footholds on a vertical face that is sheltered from prevailing winds and the glare of the midday sun. Such sites are few and far between, and one of the most ideal in the Channel is at Berry Head, a 60-metre-high promontory on the south side of Torbay. This limestone headland is a Site of Special Scientific Interest, an Area of Special Protection and a Local Nature Reserve. Its strategic situation, overlooking the safe anchorages of the bay, has also given it an impressive history. Berry Head's fortifications date back to the Iron Age, and today the ruins of a Roman wall and signs of medieval activity lie in the shadow

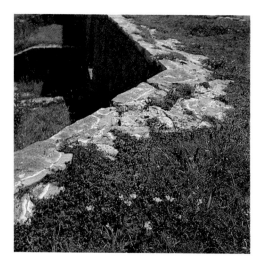

Left: *Thyme thrives on top of the dry walls of the old redoubt, a fort built during the Napoleonic wars.*

Below: *The seabird colony at Berry Head is a popular attraction for people, where the expertly-run information centre provides daily bird counts and a close up view of the ledges on live television.*

Right: *The small restharrow is a rare plant of sea cliffs, found in only a few sites in southern Britain.*

Below right: *The limestone flora of these cliffs combine rare and common flowers in a display not found elsewhere in the country.*

of eighteenth-century forts. These are a legacy from the conflict for American independence and the later Napoleonic wars. An old quarry also serves as a reminder of past days, when attempts were made to take the headland away piece by piece. Now the area is run by the borough council as a successful country park with a popular visitor centre. There, people can watch in safety and shelter a television showing views from a camera installed halfway down the cliff. This gives a gull's-eye view of the main seabird colony and enables visitors to zoom in on the most intimate antics of the birds, while the adjacent cliffs provide a vantage point to enjoy the overall scene.

Guillemots in smart suits crowd the ledges in summer, looking like Britain's answer to the penguin. These auks occur in great numbers, up to 800 at peak times. Berry Head is their most southerly mainland colony in Britain, the largest along this coast and, at present, the only one growing in size. As early as midwinter, after four or five months spent at sea, guillemots gather on the cliffs near where they intend to breed. Their numbers are erratic at this time of the year, climbing into the hundreds on one day and plummeting to zero the next. Towards winter's end they flock more consistently on the calm seas below the cliffs, amid growing activity. People on the cliff tops gain a grandstand view of the mass ceremonial movements far below. The birds weave and patter over the surface, before suddenly diving and appearing to continue underwater. Then, taking to the air, the flock wheels and dives in dramatic prelude to the breeding months ahead.

As spring passes, the remaining limestone ledges fill up and by summer a jostling band of guillemots is packed wing to wing, occupying every suitable site. The updraft carries the rising crescendo of their calls, a continuous 'arrr', backed by a growling chorus, which echoes from the surrounding walls. Guillemots build no nest, trusting that the pear shape of their single egg will prevent it rolling off the cliff. When the egg hatches after some thirty days, the chick's position is, to say the least, precarious. If it strays too far or falls on to a ledge below, it will get a hostile reception from other guillemots. And if a young chick tumbles into the sea, it is unlikely to survive because gulls are quick to spot a struggling lone youngster. However, fed on a diet of sand eels and other small fish, the chicks that survive develop fast and rapidly put on weight.

After just eighteen days, usually on a tranquil evening in July, the guillemot fledglings make a dramatic twilight leap. Although not yet able to fly, they half glide, half flutter down to the sea below, where they join the adults. Paddling fast, the flotilla leaves the headland under the cover of dark and moves out to the ground swell of the Atlantic. Here young guillemots have a better chance of survival than close inshore amid scavenging seagulls. At first their food is brought to them, but as the weeks pass they learn the skills of surface diving that enable them to catch their own meals. Underwater, the birds use their wings to propel themselves at remarkably high speed, twisting and turning in pursuit of silvery shoals of fish. Then, more than three weeks after jumping, the juveniles begin to take flight.

The cliff fronts at Berry Head are home to many other birds, including nesting colonies of kittiwakes, shags, fulmars and gulls. Above, on the tops, wheatears and whitethroats, strutting crows and noisy flocks of jackdaws fly around the fortress walls. The material used for the building blocks of the forts is also the foundation for the soil and surrounding flora. Limestone is rare in this part of England, and the headland forms an island oasis for lime-loving plants and animals. As is typical in such areas, the soil is rather shallow yet rich in humus, and contains calcium in abundance but is often strangely lacking in other nutrients such as potassium, phosphorus, nitrogen and iron. This, combined with the effects of salt spray, discourages rapid plant growth, and favours small lime-tolerant species. In places, a nibbling horde of rabbits keep the grasses well mown.

Throughout the year the flora displays a fine collection of the common and the very scarce. Around the forts and out on the cliff edge, many areas are blue with viper's bugloss. Sturdy stems of pink tree mallow, thrift and red valerian stand out against the deep blue of the sea beyond. Bee orchids grow concealed in thick grass, while other orchids bloom out in the open. There are also five extremely rare plants, some of which are found in only a handful of sites in Britain. The small hare's-ear and small rest-harrow are as diminutive as their names suggest, and the honewort, found only in the West Country, has flowers that are not much bigger. The delicate white rock-rose, with fluttering petals, grows on the sunniest slopes, while the goldilocks aster hides its striking yellow blooms, borne on solid little stems, among the rocks.

Thriving on the diversity of flowers are insects, some of which are restricted to areas of calcareous soils. One such is the adonis blue butterfly, whose caterpillar feeds on the locally common horseshoe vetch and other similar plants. Some thirty different species of butterflies and fourteen types of day-flying moths are to be found on the headland during the summer, many feeding on the lush growth flourishing in the shelter of the fortress walls. On the warmest days, grasshoppers and crickets throb from the steep slopes, where the wind carries away the sounds of people playing on the clifftops and walking along the coastal paths. Care is needed on some of the stretches of path because the

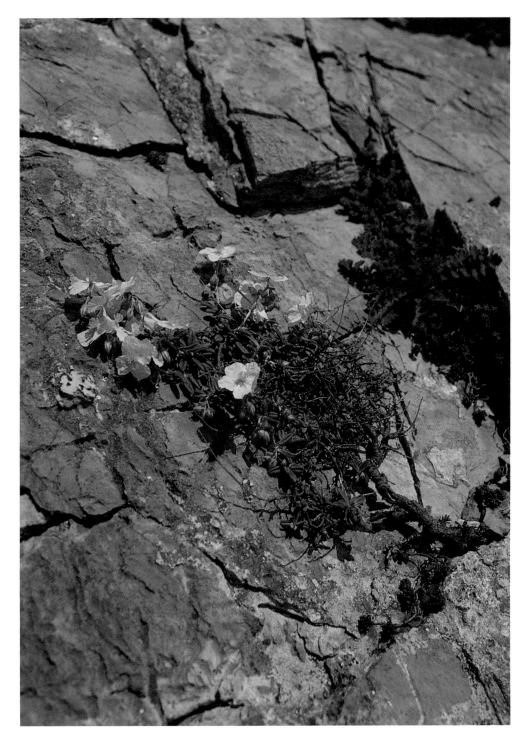

Left: *The bright yellow flowers of the goldilocks aster are a real rarity of limestone cliffs.* **Above:** *The white rock-rose is virtually confined to the sea cliffs of Somerset and South Devon.*

cliffs are sheer. Another potential danger of the place is shy and usually keeps well clear of heavy feet. Living close to the ground, the adder relies on vibration rather than sound to warn it of approaching danger.

The most common snake in Britain, the adder is easily recognised by its squat and rather thickset body with a wide zigzag stripe running down its back. It looks larger than it really is; few adders exceed 600 millimetres in length. The females are usually larger and browner in colour than the males. Both sexes spend the winter underground in burrows made by small mammals, and emerge from hibernation in March or later to hunt for mice and shrews or lizards. It is thought that each adder tends to keep to small mammals or reptiles, but all will take a variety of other prey. Fledglings of ground-nesting birds are always at risk, and earthworms and slugs may be eaten. Sometimes, adders are active hunters, sliding effortlessly through the undergrowth, exploring burrows and scenting the ground and air with their flicking forked tongue. At other times, they wait patiently for prey to come within striking distance. Whichever strategy they employ, their venom is lethal. Several minutes after striking, the snake follows the victim's scent trail to where the body lies, and swallows the animal whole. The venom is highly toxic and is only used in defence as a last resort. But when disturbed by a dog, trodden or picked up, the adder will bite. Domestic animals are frequently bitten on the head and people occasionally around the ankle or on the leg. The venom can kill small animals, but fatalities among humans are rare. Adders should, however, be treated with the greatest respect and avoided at all times, especially in the spring when their courtship is at its peak and these reptiles are at their most lively.

Sun-loving creatures, adders spend many hours basking in a warm quiet spot, and it is then that they are at their most vulnerable from the air. Birds, including buzzards and kestrels, will pounce on small snakes. Even without a breeze, the kestrel can hover over the steep slopes, scanning the ground with an intense staring gaze. The resolving power of its eyes, and those of other birds of prey, is extraordinary. Like us the kestrel has binocular vision and sees a colourful, wide, detailed view of the world, but there the similarity ends. Birds of prey possess a particularly sensitive section in the centre of the eye, which gives a slightly magnified view with greater definition. To use this effectively, the bird must keep its head still, even in flight. The technique can be seen most clearly when a bird of prey is sitting on a gently moving branch with its eyes focused on a subject. Its body seems to move almost independently of the head, which appears to be fixed to the sky.

In practice, a hunting kestrel hovers high at first until it sees a telltale sign of movement. It drops lower over the prey's last known location and as the intended victim moves again, the bird drops even closer. When just 5 or 6 metres away, the kestrel waits for the moment to strike, wings rotating above its incredibly steady head. Eyes down, it plunges into the grass, at the last moment swinging its feet round to the position just occupied by the head. The prey is grasped with outstretched talons and killed quickly since birds cannot risk damage to their delicate flight feathers.

The kestrels at Berry Head are residents, nesting within crevices in rocks. Hunting along the nearby cliff tops provides ample food, small birds, mice, shrews, beetles and worms making up the bulk of their diet. Later in the summer, grasshoppers and crickets feature high on the menu. Although the smallest insects are likely to be no more than a snack for a kestrel, the great green bush cricket makes a main course on its own. The biggest of its kind in Britain, it grows up to 50 millimetres in length, and is not uncommon in southern England, especially near the coast.

Even bigger birds, the ravens, will turn to insects when other food is not available. The cronking call of the raven in flight is a familiar sound along this coastline. Its usual ponderous progress in the air is transformed in spring when it performs exuberant and entertaining aerobatic displays. Tumbling high above, the birds roll and dive with wings half closed and for short distances even fly upside down. These aerial antics may be part of their courtship, although on the ground this is quite a ritual. Ruffling neck feathers, bowing and neck-stretching are features of the display between pairs which can mate for life.

Within a pair's territory, there may be more than one suitable site for a nest. Some ravens seem to move each year while others remain faithful to a particular place. The position of the nest is chosen with care, and trees appear to be a second choice after cliffs. In their prime location, they choose a wide inaccessible ledge high above the sea and on it build a substantial cup of sticks and sometimes seaweed stems cemented with mud and moss. The inside is lined with a deep layer of sheep's wool or hair in which the female lays a clutch of four to six pale green or blue eggs. The first signs of hatching come at around nineteen days, and the chicks are closely guarded. Although capable of flight after six weeks they often remain around the home cliffs.

Commonly thought of as scavengers, ravens do feed principally on the remains of dead sheep and rabbits, but will supplement this diet with small birds, and even fruit and seeds. Also, they are not averse to taking any fish that may be washed on to the shore below. Ravens were once to be found throughout

Above: *The male kestrel, like his mate, is frequently to be seen taking advantage of the updraught from the cliffs, hovering in search of prey.*

Right: *The adder is Britain's only venomous snake. They are common along the coast where they can be seen basking in the sun.*

Britain, but are now largely confined to the cliffs and crags in the west and north of the country, and the south-west of England is a stronghold. One survey discovered the high breeding density of fifteen pairs along a 27-kilometre stretch of coastline in Devon and Cornwall.

Pigeons have come to exploit many habitats and food supplies, and, measured in terms of number and spread, they are successful. The ubiquitous multi-coloured flocks of these birds, which today plague city centres, are the free-living descendants of captive-bred stock. The rock dove was originally domesticated 5000 years ago for its flesh, and some escapees interbred with their wild relatives. Today feral birds, closely resembling the ancestral rock dove, fly and forage around many cliffs. The pressures of natural selection have once again favoured the duller wild coloration and wary habit. But brightly coloured pigeons, sitting or wheeling around in flocks, are tempting targets for the most daring pirate that patrols these shores.

From a distance of a kilometre or more, the peregrine can pick out a pigeon winging its way over the cliff. To the pigeon, the falcon appears little more than a speck in the clear blue sky, its remoteness belying its intention. Gathering speed, the predator dives in a spectacular stoop, near vertical with wings almost closed, and in seconds it has struck the victim a stunning blow with its talons. The peregrine is a sky raider without equal and, of all the birds of prey, it became the falconer's most prized possession. The larger female is known as the falcon, and the male as a tiercel. In the past, the exclusive right to fly such a bird became the privilege of earls, princes and kings. Severe penalties punished any transgressor, so wild birds were effectively given noble protection.

The invention of the shotgun during the eighteenth century put paid to the peregrine's importance as the hunting companion for game. Persecution by gamekeepers and pigeon fanciers then took its toll, probably more so than today because the eggs as well as the birds themselves were destroyed. The Victorians' passion for collecting added to the burden. Many lifeless, glassy-eyed peregrines soon peered from glass cases, and entire clutches of eggs ended up being hidden in drawers, their embryos stifled. But peregrines were not so badly hit as some other raptors, judging from the records of their nests. Clifftop eyries are traditional and in some cases occupation can be traced back to medieval times. Out of forty-nine sites known between the sixteenth and nineteenth centuries, forty-one were in use before the outbreak of the Second World War.

Although peregrines take a wide range of prey, from tiny goldcrests to mallards and rabbits, pigeons are high on their hit list. Unfortunately, during the war this brought them into conflict with the military, which used homing pigeons to carry secret messages. It became official policy to destroy peregrines and, although killed throughout the country, it was on the south coast that most avian casualties were inflicted. Their population was more than halved, about 600 were killed and many eggs and nests destroyed in the cause of national interests. In the decade that followed the peace in 1945, peregrine numbers increased to almost pre-war levels, around 700 pairs. Then came another crash. For reasons at first unknown, birds failed to lay, or laid eggs with thin shells that broke in the nest or were infertile. Their breeding failure continued across Britain, the population reaching an all-time low in the mid-1960s. In Cornwall the peregrine, which had been practically wiped out during wartime, had reoccupied at least seventeen of its twenty known sites by 1955, but no birds bred there in 1960. An improvement was eventually noticed when partial bans on pesticides began to take effect during the 1970s. Today it is recognised that, as in the case of the otter, highly persistent organochlorine pesticides pass through the food chain and accumulate in the tissues of top predators, such as peregrines, and people.

Today, the peregrine population is back to its previous strength and the birds are nesting in most of their former strongholds. Their ability to return to exactly the same ledges after an interval of several years, and perhaps many generations, may seem extraordinary to us. But peregrines probably have a strongly inherited sense of where to nest. The prime consideration is perhaps inaccessibility to disturbance or danger within a hunting territory, offering a degree of shelter. While other birds may have a much wider choice, the options open to a peregrine are limited on an exposed rocky cliff. So when a pair measure their requirements against various sites only one may fit, and that will tend to be a traditional eyrie.

The birds are resident all year, each pair holding a territory which depends on the terrain but generally stretches some 6 kilometres along the coast. As spring approaches they perform energetic aerial displays, diving and swooping together. During courtship the male feeds his mate continuously, both in the air, and on the chosen ledge. There they bow to each other, chittering as they do so. The ceremony is thought to reinforce the pair's bond and overcome the female's natural aggression, for the male is much smaller and could easily become her next meal. The nest is just a scrape or the abandoned remnants of another bird's, such as the raven which chooses similar sites. Three or four eggs are generally produced at intervals of forty-eight to seventy-eight hours and in southern Britain are usually laid by the second week in April. The young begin hatching around thirty days later in the order in which they were laid.

Above: *Ravens are among the earliest nesting birds and these young will be flying when six weeks old.* **Below:** *The male peregrine is known as the tiercel and in common with other birds of prey is smaller than his mate.* **Right:** *South Devon. Steep cliffs and sheltered coves make the south-west coastline of the English Channel ideal peregrine and raven country.*

At first, the young peregrines are clad in white down. After about ten days they grow another layer which makes them appear big and fluffy, as if swaddled in a white fur coat, as they sit on their ledge. The second layer keeps the young warm and frees the female to hunt for her brood. At twenty-one days old their flight feathers are beginning to grow and they are trying out their wings. They can leave the ledge any time after thirty-five days, but remain close by because their parents continue to return to the nesting ledge with food. By then competition is intense and carcasses are eagerly stripped. There are few birds that peregrines will not tackle, especially in defence of their young. Ravens are harried at every opportunity, yet often nest surprisingly close by. Even dogs and people need to take care when the female begins hunting for her young.

In the air the peregrine is in a power class of its own, but for sheer mastery of the winds a relative newcomer to these shores is unsurpassed. The fulmar is a bird of the open seas, hardly ever stepping a webbed foot on land, except during the breeding season. Its effortless, gliding, stiff-winged flight serves it well on its ocean wanderings, saving energy as it rides the air currents above the undulating swell. Before the nineteenth century, the fulmar was a stranger to British shores. A bird more used to arctic seas, its only outpost in the temperate waters of the North Atlantic was on the remote island of St Kilda in the Outer Hebrides. Then in 1878, after colonising Icelandic cliffs and the Faroes, fulmars began breeding in Shetland, on Foula. Since then the explosion in their numbers and range has continued, and they have spread right around the coast of Britain. By 1934 they were nesting on the south coast after several years of prospecting, and in 1949 took up residence at Berry Head. In recent years they have also spread across the Channel to France.

Fulmars feed while paddling about, eating a variety of plankton, such as floating crustaceans, worms and pelagic snails. They can dive from the surface, with wings partly closed, to depths of several metres in search of small fish. They are also a familiar sight scavenging discarded offal from trawlers far out to sea, and the growth of the fishing industry during the last century is thought to have helped their advance. But that may be only part of the story. It has been suggested that the fulmar's success is an example of evolution in action. From the lottery of the bird's genes, a vigorous individual emerged that was ancestor to a new breed, perhaps better adapted to exploiting the vast amounts of bigger plankton that thrive in warmer waters than the arctic. Young birds especially are at risk from seasonal shortages. A shift in the fulmar's natural food or a change in its feeding habit, aided at certain times by fish offal, may have reduced the risk of shortages, giving the new breed a major advantage. Whatever the reasons, it is estimated that today there are well over 300 000 pairs nesting in British waters alone. Since the fulmar is slow to mature, and each pair normally raises only one chick a year, this population boom is amazing.

The fulmar, together with shearwaters, albatrosses and some other seabirds, belongs to an order which probably contains more individuals than any other. The birds in the order are called tubenoses because they have tubular nostrils mounted on the bill. Far from simple adornments, the tubes make the birds' nasal senses highly acute. They are thought to use the nostrils partly to gauge the subtle strengths of air-flows, and partly to detect odours at great distance, a feat at which fulmars apparently excel.

Fulmars breed from May until September, on a sheltered ledge or in a hole high up a cliff. A hollow in the rock, or on any turf that is present, serves as a nest for the single white egg. Incubation is a long lonely affair and the male takes the first sitting, which lasts around ten days, while the female feeds far out to sea. Her return marks his departure, and the pair continue to alternate their duties. After fifty-three days the young fulmar hatches and is closely attended by a parent for the first few weeks. It takes nearly two months for the fledgling to develop sufficiently to be able to fly. Then it launches itself from the cliff, trusting its future to chance and the wind. Fulmars are faithful birds, keeping the same mate and nest site year after year. One couple is known to have remained together for twenty-seven years and others for as much as forty, the older more experienced pairs having the greatest success in rearing their young.

The fulmar's forte is riding the upcurrent of the cliff. Only when this is seen in slow motion can the full beauty of the bird's dynamic trimming be seen. Constant twitches of its tail and fine adjustment of the wings enable it to hang in mid-air. Then, tail up, the fulmar falls away in a banking dive, its wingtips almost touching the steep face as it sweeps along the cliff. Wheeling around, the bird repeats its path, rising as if to land, before turning again. Such is the elegance and meek appearance of the fulmar that the strength of its defence comes as a surprise. Any intruders at a colony risk being greeted with a foul-smelling oily fluid, ejected from the bird's mouth. This deterrent is highly effective, as anyone unfortunate enough to get caught in its spray will testify. But just how potent it is only became apparent when the closed-circuit television camera on the cliff face at Berry Head recorded an extraordinary confrontation between a fulmar and a falcon.

That year, a female peregrine had laid her clutch of eggs in a sheltered hollow in the cliff. In previous years a pair of fulmars had occupied the site, and earlier in the season they had again shown considerable interest in the cave. It was

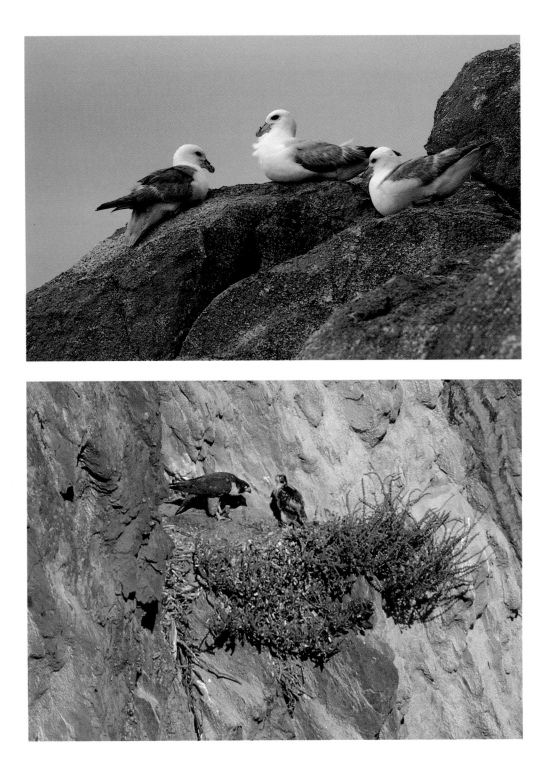

thought that the peregrines' appearance had put paid to their plans. However, over the next few days, the fulmars paid regular visits to the peregrines' nest. The tiercel was young and this was probably his first mate and year of breeding. By the end of the first week, when he was sitting, the sudden appearance of the fulmars, cackling and spitting at the cave entrance, caused him to leave. In response his mate chased and appeared to chastise him for deserting his post.

The female peregrine was bigger and bolder, a mature and experienced falcon, and she sat tight on the nest as the fulmars fearlessly confronted her face to face. Lowering her wings she covered the nest, protecting her precious clutch of eggs from the evil oil being spat. On occasions the commotion attracted other fulmars to the fray, and up to ten birds were counted at the entrance. Then the two main contenders launched an all-out attack and the peregrine was pushed to the back of the cave. The fights frequently reached screaming point as she defended herself time and again, flying forward with wings spread, lethal talons held high, flailing at the aggressors while sitting back on her tail. After a few weeks of being at the receiving end of the fulmar's foul mouth, her beautiful plumage began to suffer. Her formerly white breast feathers were filthy, and her wings were badly soiled by the fulmar's evil-smelling stomach oil. Eventually, with just one more week to hatching, the peregrine falcon deserted, leaving the nest and its chilling eggs to be pushed aside.

The fulmars nested successfully that year, rearing a healthy chick. The female peregrine found her way down the coast to Plymouth, where she was rescued barely alive on a beach. Her plumage was so badly caked that she could not hunt and was dying from starvation. At first it was thought that she was another casualty of marine pollution. Then, when her feathers defied cleaning with the usual preparations, she was recognised as being the bird from Berry Head. As the weeks passed, with expert care and feeding, she regained her lost strength, but the state of her plumage could improve only after moulting. In due course, she will one day return to grace the Channel cliffs again with her spectacular stoops and chanting cry. But whether this particular peregrine will ever tangle with a fulmar again, only time will tell.

Above left: *Fulmars are relative newcomers to Channel shores. Even until the mid-twentieth century they were a rare northern visitor.* **Below:** *The traditional eyrie of the peregrine, its nest, may have been used by generations of these birds, perhaps for several centuries.*

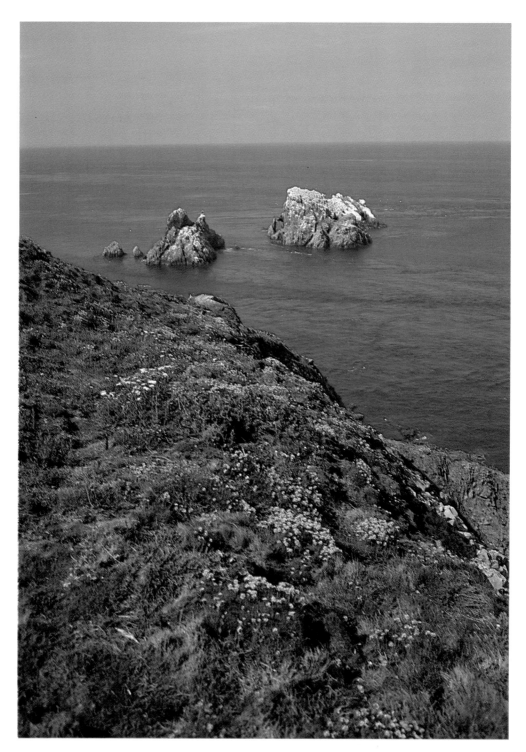

The finest view of a gannet colony in western Europe can be gained from the cliffs of Alderney which overlook Les Etacs, otherwise known as the Garden Rocks.

CHAPTER FIVE

The Channel Islands

Not far from the Channel's mainland coasts are scattered hard rocks. Many are little more than mariners' nightmares, rearing their jagged heads just clear of the tide. Others are much larger, miniature continents complete with a natural history unique to their shores. A few are remote rocky fortresses. Free from disturbance by people and ground-living predators, these islands are a great attraction to creatures that roam the sea, yet must return to land to breed. The gannet is the biggest bird in the North Atlantic and over 70 per cent of the world's population hatch in the British Isles. Their southernmost colony in Europe, lying just off the north coast of Brittany, is the only one in France. Île Rouzic, the largest of Les Sept Îles, contains over 4500 gannets during the breeding season. It is not, however, the only colony in the Channel. To the north-east, no more than a couple of hours as the gannet flies, lie two more white splashed stacks off Alderney. This is the most northerly of the Channel Islands, an archipelago which includes Guernsey and Jersey.

At its closest, the archipelago is situated less than 100 kilometres south of England and only 12 kilometres from the coast of Normandy. Although the Channel Islands swear allegiance to the English Crown, they are geographically part of the continent and enjoy a near Mediterranean climate. Their culture, too, owes almost as much to the French as to the English, and their wildlife is a startling blend of the common and the exotic. As might be expected, the largest islands contain the greatest number of different plants and animals. However, even these islands are relatively small. If they could be walked across at their widest point in a straight line, Alderney would be traversed in a little more than an hour. Guernsey would take around two and a half hours and Jersey nearly four.

The islands were formed hesitantly during the final flooding of the Channel some 6000 years ago, after the end of the last ice age. Considerable differences in the depths of the surrounding seas meant that some pieces of higher ground were isolated from the Continent long before others. As the ocean levels rose gradually, Guernsey and its associated islands, Herm and Sark, were the first to sever their land link and Alderney soon followed. Jersey maintained its connection much longer, but that too was eventually drowned. Precisely when the final break came is unknown, but for much of the islands' natural history it was crucial. The successive waves of plants and animals that had spread slowly north in the wake of the retreating ice were then halted on the mainland coast. Only seeds carried by birds or the wind could cross the tidal barrier. Birds and insects incapable of long flights were prevented from colonising the new islands and mammals could no longer walk there. Long-distance travellers, the migrant birds, butterflies and bats, were not so limited.

On islands, evolutionary change is fast. Animals and plants left in isolation do not all remain the same in succeeding generations. To begin with, the variations are small. In all living organisms, tiny changes may occur in the genes during the intricacies of reproduction, resulting in differences or mutations in the offspring. Within small isolated communities, such mutations have less chance of being overwhelmed and diluted than they would in larger populations. In consequence, any changes in anatomy or behaviour that do not endanger life are more likely to be passed on to future generations.

In the Channel Islands, a brief 6000 years or more of isolation has been enough to allow the evolution of a few distinct island races. The wood mouse here differs slightly from its mainland counterpart, being bigger and more brightly coloured. Guernsey has a short-tailed field vole, which is found on none of the other islands. Jersey has its own bank vole, which is sufficiently different from all other races to be considered a separate subspecies.

More puzzling is how two different types of shrews came to survive on separate islands. The white-toothed shrew lives only on Alderney and Guernsey, and is slightly smaller than its continental cousin. In contrast, the lesser white-toothed shrew is found on Jersey and Sark, although it too is not native to Britain or found closer than 320 kilometres away in France.

Comparatively recently, people have introduced other life. Some were brought intentionally, while others were accidental, creatures that jumped ship, were transported in goods or carried on a hairy body. Seeds especially travel easily in this way. The Channel Islands' contact with humans has also provided homes for some animals. The empty fortifications that still stand in silent witness to several hundred years of European conflict and two World Wars, are today inhabited by seabirds and bats.

In terms of the abundance and diversity of plant life, the Channel Islands is without equal in Britain. Around 1800 different species of plants are packed into an area of less than 195 square kilometres. This is three to four times the average density found on the British mainland. The islands' immense floral diversity is due partly to their rich variety of habitats and to the nutrients in their soils. The islands are mainly composed of granite, but limitations in the underlying geology are compensated for in other ways. Chalk is not present, but deposits of calcium-rich seashells enrich several areas. Also the influence of the ocean stretches far inland, not just on the salt-laden winds, but in the tonnes of seaweed that have for centuries fertilised the land.

The cliff tops are a botanist's delight. April finds the short turf displaying tiny sand crocus blooms, so small they can only be appreciated by grovelling on the sunniest days. A little larger, but surely one of the islands' most ephemeral flowers, is that of the annual spotted rock-rose. It opens briefly in the bright morning sun, only to shed its yellow petals by early afternoon. Far longer lasting is the colourful broom that sprawls across the south-western cliffs. Its prostrate state is not due to wind-levelling but a real adaptation to the severe conditions that prevail on weather-blasted cliffs. In places such as Alderney, where it paints the cliffs yellow, it has a constant companion. The broomrape is a parasitic plant that grows only on the broom. Another yellow-flowered plant of the cliffs rarely seen in the British Isles is the golden samphire. Not as widespread or spectacular as the low-growing broom, it is to be found on the four largest islands, but only seems to be increasing in Guernsey. One plant that is having no problem invading the cliffs is a garden escapee belonging to the huge family known commonly as mesembryanthemums. The kaffir fig, with large fleshy leaves and bright pink or yellow flowers, is a native of South Africa, which is now running wild on the islands, forming dense heavy carpets hanging over the rocks. Indeed, its success is beginning to threaten less vigorous plants, by smothering.

Sand dunes are an extensive feature of the Channel Islands' west coasts, and most have undergone irreversible change. Jersey has one of the biggest, stretching inland of St Ouen's bay. Here, as elsewhere in low-lying areas, sea and wartime defences have effectively cut the dunes off from the beach. But even deprived of their major source of sand, the dunes have managed to retain the essence of their wild identity and fascination. Tough stands of prickly-leaved sea holly defy the growing number of trampling feet, and sea lavender grows in thick beds. Far more rare is the pink-flowered great sea stock, which today is only found rising in sandy seclusion on the dunes. Globes of pink sea thrift are common around the coast, but on Jersey another taller form reaches one of its northern outposts. The Jersey thrift is a native of the Mediterranean and southern shores.

Far left: *Clonque Bay, Alderney, the most northerly and third largest of the Channel Islands. It has a rugged, wild beauty which is rich in wild flowers and is a haven for seabirds.* **Above left:** *The Jersey bank vole is unique to the island, a truly endemic creature, which is as much at home in woodlands and hedgebank as in the rough grasslands and gorse of the coast.* **Centre left:** *The Glanville fritillary butterfly, which is a real rarity in Britain, can be commonly encountered on the island's cliffs in early summer.* **Below:** *The Green lizard is a continental reptile which failed to reach Britain before the flooding of the Channel. Found on both Guernsey and Jersey, it is not as common as it once was.*

Another inhabitant of shingle and sand is related to one of the most tasty vegetables. The wild sea kale, however, is much tougher. Its knee-high mound of large grey-green leaves are enveloped in a mass of white flowers from June. The arrival of these petals signals the start of a slow-moving invasion. Snails make their way across the sand and swarm over the plants. In some places capable of withstanding extremes of heat and drought, these Pisan snails are native to Italy, first identified near Pisa, and are thought to have been introduced into the Channel Islands in the nineteenth century. Despite their Mediterranean origins, they retreat into their shells during the heat of the day. It is then, when they are huddled in clusters, that the remarkable variations in their shell patterns can best be seen.

Beyond the seafront and steep freshly-formed dunes, the older, more stable sands have their own distinct pattern of life. Here hare's-tail grass shakes in the wind and burnet roses hug the ground, protecting their creamy white flowers from the sea breeze. The burnet is a dwarf rose that scents the air in June and spreads by suckers, forming extensive prickly patches. As midday temperatures soar, the air vibrates with the chirruping calls of grasshoppers and crickets. If you walk across some areas, grasshoppers seem to fly at every pace. One of the most striking reveals a flash of blue wings that vanish when the insect settles. A smaller greyish brown, coastal bush-cricket is now recognised as a unique local race. Only such sun-loving creatures can survive the parched conditions, but the rewards for doing so are great. There is little competition for food in places of extremes.

The setting of the sun subdues the summer heat and the dusk brings a new louder song pulsating from the ground. Sitting in the entrance to its burrow a male field cricket repeatedly raises its brown and yellow wings. The strident sound is produced by a zigzag movement, as its right forewing is scraped over its left. Special stridulating structures then amplify the noise, which can be heard up to 50 metres away. So pleasant are the soothing vibrations of the field cricket that in the south of France they are kept as family pets just for their song. However, the purpose of the call is not to amuse but to declare territory and attract a likely mate. Advertising its position seems a rash act for a creature as edible as a cricket, but the high-pitched call is surprisingly difficult to locate, and it can always retreat into its burrow.

By summer, the coast is alive with many insects other than the jumping kind. Butterflies are frequently seen and are worthy of a second glance, for in the Channel Islands few creatures are what they at first appear. A butterfly that looks more like a moth, with its wings folded at rest, may initially be identified as a small skipper. But closer investigation will reveal it to be an Essex skipper, a real rarity in Britain. Another butterfly, only reaching as far north as the Isle of Wight, also frequents the flower-filled gullies on Channel Island cliffs. The Glanville fritillary butterfly, with colourful orange-chequered wings, spends the first part of its life as a black hairy caterpillar. Its consuming passion for the leaves of the buckthorn and sea plantain confines it to the coast.

The Jersey tiger is the boldest flying insect of all, standing out in its near black and cream stripes. Although it tracks down its meals using sight and smell, this day-flying moth is quite harmless for it feeds on the nectar of flowers. Its striped upper wings and brilliant orange underwings are its brightest feature and last line of defence. Both serve to surprise a predator and warn of its unpalatable taste. Jersey tigers occur across the southern European continent, but have only a toehold in Britain. Apart from the Channel Islands, they are common along the coast of south Devon, from Seaton to Torbay. Another day-flying moth, more common and equally well marked, is the six-spot burnet. Low flying, hovering and dashing, it too relies on its distastefulness and warning coloration of darkest green and deep red.

One of the strangest groups of insects, the ant-lions, is mainly confined to the tropics. However, some members occur further north, such as one species found in only a few locations on the warm west coast of Jersey. Although in the air the gauzy winged flight of the adult resembles a damselfly, it is brown with mottled wings. Ant-lions are closely related to the delicate lacewings, which also have carnivorous larvae, but there the similarities end. The ant-lion larva lives in sandy soil, where it begins by constructing a small pit. Grains of sand are hurled from the hole by a flick of its head. The larva then buries itself at the bottom and waits with only its strong jaws protruding from the centre. The trap it has set is deadly simple in design. When a foraging ant falls over the rim and attempts to climb back out, the sides of the pit are at a critical angle, so that each movement starts an avalanche of sand. Below, the ant-lion larva energetically flicks a steady shower of grains up over the victim's head, hampering its efforts to escape. The ant tries frantically to struggle up the cascading slope, but eventually falls back exhausted. Then the larva seizes its prey and drags it out of sight before sucking it dry. A year later, at Midsummer, the larva finally pupates hidden beneath the soil, safe in its spherical cocoon. Six weks later, it finally emerges as a winged adult.

The warmth of summer also brings reptiles to more active life, including the continental green lizard. This striking beast is covered in brilliant scales giving it a viridescent and black speckled sheen. It may be found lounging in the sun

Right: *The annual rock-rose sheds its petals around midday.*
Centre: *The low-growing prostrate broom colours many of the islands' south-west cliffs in early summer.*
Below: *Greater broomrape thrives only on prostrate broom.*
Far right: *Ox-eye daisy and thrift, Alderney. The seabird sanctuary of Burhou Island lies beyond.*

only in the hottest parts of Guernsey and Jersey. Fully mature males typically have a blue throat, green back and yellowish underside, while the females are often more mottled and sometimes almost brown. Both sexes hunt by sight, sometimes scurrying among the dry grass stalking their insect prey and at other times, waiting in ambush. The final move is always a fast snatch with reptilian jaws.

Some lizards move with less speed, such as the slow-worms found on all three of the largest islands. The only other lizard to be seen is restricted to a well-known corner of Jersey. Sunbathing on the battlements and slopes surrounding Gorey Castle, the wall lizard is aptly named. It is not particularly widespread on the island and this fortress really is its stronghold. When the stonework around the castle is repointed, gaps are left to give these attractively marked lizards somewhere safe to hide. A few hours after the sun has risen over the Gulf of St Malo, the lizards emerge to bask above the oblivious tourists below. Wall lizards are accomplished climbers and common on the mainland continent. They occur right across southern and central Europe yet, like their green relatives and so many other species, failed to cross into Britain before the flooding of the Channel.

Although some fortifications built at the back of beaches effectively blocked the supplies of sand for the dunes, they did help to create new habitats by enlarging existing wetlands. The greatest limitation of the life of an island is lack of freshwater and over the years many areas on the Channel Islands have been drained. This has served to increase the importance of the remaining freshwater ponds and wetlands that are so rich in wild plants and animals. The continental loose-flowered orchid, for which the islands are well known, today survives in only a few damp meadows. There are also frogs, which differ from the species found in Britain. The agile frog has a more pointed snout than its common relative, and its longer legs are said to make it more nimble. Apart from when spawning during wet weather in the spring, the densest concentrations of frogs are discovered in late summer. By then the remaining freshwater in the shallow ponds has all but evaporated, leaving a crazy paving of mud. The shrinking dark soft centre, encroached by a ring that is already crisp and dry, creates an arena for millions of tiny flies. Crawling among the insects, lunging and licking their lips, are a hopping hoard of equally small frogs. Some still have stubby tails in the process of being absorbed, while others are perfect little adults. Eventually they have the ability to conquer dry land, and escape from the dwindling water to disperse into the grass and surrounding scrublands.

Even on the shore, the ability to ensure desiccation is vital to many of the plants and animals that survive in the intertidal zone. In the Channel Islands that region is vast and the tides are at their greatest in the south. Jersey has spring floods of 12 metres or more and so conceals much at high water. Twice daily, tiny islets and offshore rocks are revealed as the mere tips of awesome reefs. Full ebb lays bare a treacherous rocky shelf of almost unbelievable proportions. The seabed here is so shallow that if the tide fell by as much again, Jersey would once more be linked to France.

Low water leaves a rugged lunar-like landscape of jagged rocks and pools, along with their stranded life. Darting fish, hermit crabs and prawns lurk in a submarine garden of waving anemones and seaweeds. Rock, unlike mud or sand, provides a solid base for plants to establish themselves, and rocky shores are often shrouded in the algae that we dismiss as weeds. The currents around the islands denude rocks of many of the larger seaweeds. This allows a rich variety of smaller marine algae to thrive, and around Guernsey alone over 270 different species are found.

The protection afforded by a shell gives molluscs a distinct advantage in the intertidal zone. Top-shells are among the most attractive of these animals. Intolerant of mud, five varieties of top-shell thrive in these islands' clear waters. One that is found nowhere else, except along the Atlantic coast of France and Spain, is the rare flat top-shell, which lives just above the half-tide level. Another mollusc that lives in deeper water is a monster compared with the little top-shell. The ormer, for which the islands are justly famous, is related to the limpet, but its shell differs radically in design. A large muscular foot enables it to move with surprising speed across the algae-encrusted rocks upon which it grazes. At the front is its head bearing a pair of stalked eyes and a pair of tentacles. The ormer's ear-shaped shell is punctured by a row of holes, five of which are usually open. Old apertures are gradually sealed as new ones are formed at the growing edge of the shell. Sense organs protrude from the holes, which also enable the ormer to discharge sea water that has passed over its gills, along with its waste, and eggs or sperm.

Unfortunately for the ormer, it is treasured by people. The large shell is lined in mother-of-pearl, and much sought-after by souvenir hunters. Its flesh, too, is an island delicacy. So much in demand are these creatures that along the low-tide line they are few and far between. Even in deeper water they are not safe, for they are accessible to divers, although illegal on some islands. They are, however, protected during the breeding season, and there are restrictions on the minimum size to be taken. But people are not the ormer's only enemies. In

Above, top: *The name ormer is a contraction of* oreille de mer *(ear of the sea) which refers to the shape of its shell.*

Above: *Sea holly with its prickly leaves grows in sand dunes closest to the beach.*

Left: *Low water in St Ouen's Bay, Jersey, reveals a vast rocky reef. The tides here are among the greatest in the world.*

the depths beyond the lowest tides, they are preyed upon by large starfish and octopus. These animals discard the empty shells, leaving them to be dragged by currents and concentrated in the eddies.

Strong tides sweep through narrow channels, and storms drive the turbulence to the depths. In just a few places, the currents combine to dredge the bottom of its litter and a nearby beach becomes a beautiful graveyard of the deep. One such lies on the picturesque little island of Herm to the east of Guernsey. Here, millions of shells are washed ashore each year, including the descriptively named venus and tusk shells, cowries and keyhole limpets. These marvels of natural engineering survive to delight human beachcombers, long after the creatures that made them.

Other islands in these waters are Jethou, close to Herm but even smaller, while Sark lies further out. Tall with imposing sea cliffs, Sark is the fourth largest Channel Island. Every spring and autumn these islands are alive with small birds passing through while migrating north or south. Most warblers migrate rather than face the lean winter months. Since these birds are mobile, free to come and go, it is unlikely that a unique race will develop on the Channel Islands. However, they are home to one of the rarest of warblers, and this bird is a resident, feeding on insects and spiders. Dartford warblers are found on the three largest islands, and in other parts of Europe. These little birds are mainly dark, but the male has a red breast in summer and the habit of continually flicking its long tail erect. In the Mediterranean they inhabit dry scrub, while further north they frequent areas of lowland heath. Their range extends up the western seaboard of France and just reaches southern England, where their hold is extremely tenuous. The decline of their heathland home in Dorset and the New Forest has in places drastically reduced their numbers. An even bigger threat to these non-migratory birds is the cold which deprives them of their food. In the past, severe winters have taken a heavy toll, and almost wiped them out in England.

In the Channel Islands, as elsewhere, these birds are normally secretive, keeping low in the gorse. Four were found flitting around in the open at mid-morning, but then they were partly hidden in the murk of a swirling sea mist. At other times, their harsh, unmelodious call may be the only indication of their presence. However, in April, at the beginning of the breeding season, the males call and display more boldly. Dartford warblers mate for life. Their nest site, in the Channel Islands at least, tends to be in the gorse cover of cliffs and coastal valleys, often remarkably close to footpaths. The male has a curious habit of building a series of 'trial' nests, flimsy constructions which the female usually

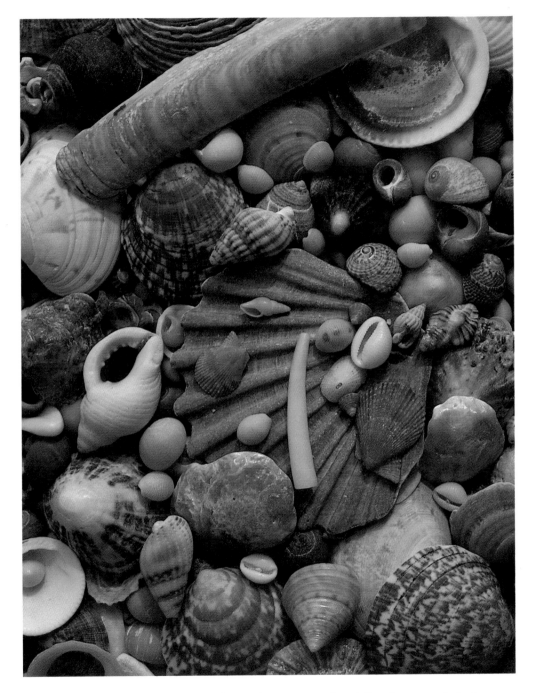

Shell beach on the little island of Herm is famous for its variety of seashells. They are washed ashore from surrounding deep water channels by strong tidal currents.

rejects. The final nest is mainly her work, a cup of plant material, grass and roots interwoven with moss and spiders' webs. The finishing touch is a lining of hair and fine plant matter. She lays three to four eggs which hatch in just twelve days, and by the end of a month the young have flown the nest. Such a quick turn-round enables a pair to produce up to three broods a year, a necessary adaptation for birds that are prone to suffer sudden heavy losses.

The Channel Islands support a large community of birds, including over ninety different species that are known to breed here. In addition to this colourful mixture of residents and regular summer visitors, there are many more for which the islands are just another port of call. Some birds may come alone or in pairs, while others descend in their thousands. Of all the island's summer visitors, the seabirds are the most eye-catching and audible. Apart from gulls, the majority of these seabirds spend the winter far to the south, and common terns are no exception. They winter off the equatorial coast of west Africa, returning in summer to breed in noisy colonies on several small islets in the Channel and further north. Wherever they gather the air is constantly filled with dancing wings and a cacophony of harsh cries.

The terns are known as the swallows of the sea because of their graceful flight and characteristic forked tail. These majestic white birds breed mainly on the islands' remote rocks and shingle reefs, but their most impressive site is man-made. Guarding the entrance to the channel between Guernsey and Herm, a grim Victorian fortress, built in 1855, rises forbiddingly above the sea. This round stone tower, which sits on the rocky islet of Bréhon, was deserted by people many years ago. A colony of common terns has now taken up raucous residence.

By early summer the upper ramparts of Bréhon tower are alive with returning terns. The courtship of the common tern involves high flying and ceremonial feeding. The male presents his intended mate with a continuous supply of small fish, generally made up of sand eels. Once the pair is established, a breeding site is chosen with care. The nest is usually a bare scrape in the sand, shingle or soil, but on the hard flat heights of the tower such digging is impossible. Also, although the central well from which the gun emplacements radiate is deep and sheltered, the birds prefer to nest on top of the wide walls and bunkers, and these slope gently towards the sea. However, plants springing from every nook and cranny solve the problems. Yellow stonecrop forms low-growing tufts in which the birds can trample a safe hollow, and brilliant stands of ox-eye daisies provide shelter from the wind. Here, settled on colourful cushions, common terns lay their clutch of two or three eggs all within a week or so of each other.

Keeping together in a colony in which breeding becomes synchronised has distinct advantages for highly visible white birds. Losses of eggs and young were found to be relatively constant throughout the season, even though their numbers increased dramatically for a short time. So a higher proportion of a thousand eggs laid in a week will survive to hatch than the same number laid over, say, four weeks, and the greater number of chicks will also be relatively safer. Although the earliest breeders are likely to suffer greater losses, the colony as a whole benefits. The terns' colonies also allow the birds more effective defence. High on top of a tower or isolated rock the only predators are likely to be other birds, particularly great black-backed and herring gulls which are always on the lookout for an unattended egg or young. Mobbing by the colony helps deter any potential predators and limit the losses. This is a tactic at which terns excel, as anyone who has strayed near a colony will attest. Dive-bombing and screaming their anger, they have even been known to draw blood from an unwary person's head. Gathering together can have the drawback of increased competition for feeding, but it has been suggested that membership of a tern colony actually improves each bird's chances of finding food. This is especially so where birds seek out a nomadic prey, such as shoals of fish that may move from hour to hour, let alone day to day. Individuals returning from a particular direction carrying food would indicate where the best shoals of fish are to be found. Colonies also help young birds breeding for the first time to learn the location of a safe site.

The parent terns share the incubation of the eggs for twenty-three days. The eggs, laid at intervals of one or two days, hatch in the same order. The first sign of hatching comes from within as the chick punctures the airspace inside and begins to call. The parents undoubtedly hear this and respond by being particularly attentive, but no seabird actually assists its offspring to emerge. As the chick dries, its mottled down becomes fluffy, rendering it difficult for a gull to swallow. The parent quickly removes the empty shell, because broken shells are likely to draw the attention of sharp-eyed predators to a meal. Within three days, when all the young have hatched, the parents and young leave the nest, and the chicks hide close by while the adults search widely for food.

In some places, they travel considerable distances for food but in the shallow warm waters around the islands, shoals of sand eels are easy to find. The birds hover on quivering wings before plunging into the sea and picking fish from just below the surface. When they return to the nest, the chicks appear from the safety of their floral hideouts to be given fish almost as long as themselves. After three weeks their adult feathers are forming and by the end of a month they are capable of flight. Once that first, most vulnerable stage is behind them,

Left: *Bréhon tower, built in 1855, is today defended only by the terns that nest on its ramparts.*

Above: *The common tern is one of the island's most attractive summer-visiting seabirds.*

they must learn the flying and hunting skills they will need to survive. But breeding in colonies, and flying and feeding in flocks, they are unlikely to be on their own.

The tides that rip past these islands are notorious hazards to shipping, yet profit the wildlife. The strong flows carry abundant supplies of food, while dangerous currents and terrifying waves leave the outer islands undisturbed. Alderney has infamous waters, and the tidal flow, known as the Swinge, that pours between the little island of Burhou and the harbour is one of the worst. The strength of its currents was once underestimated by the British Admiralty. In 1864, a new kilometre-long breakwater was completed, a masterpiece of Victorian building. Within six months the far end was breached and after eight years most of it had been swept away. Today, the breakwater is little more than half the original length, and loads equivalent to 100 tonnes of stone each day have to be deposited on the seaward side to prevent that from being destroyed. So piece by piece, Alderney is being thrown into the Swinge.

Even in the calmest weather, this stretch of sea is rife with broken water. A great belt of standing waves known as the overfalls is caused by the tidal spate streaming over the rugged seabed. In rough weather the Swinge is filled with magnificent white-crested waves. The island of Burhou, lying to one side, is the largest part of a rugged reef that stretches to the Casquets lighthouse. It takes less than fifteen minutes to walk this tiny island from end to end and less than five minutes to cover its width. Even its highest point is no more than 25 metres above sea level. However, Burhou has an importance out of all proportion to its size, because it is home to the largest colony of puffins still to be found in the English Channel.

In previous centuries, the population of puffins in the Channel's western approaches could be counted in their tens of thousands. Even in the early 1950s, more than 100 000 puffins could regularly be seen floating in huge rafts close to the shore. By 1968 that number had reduced to 40 000, by 1975 to no more than 2000, and just three years later the colony had dwindled to a pitiful 200 birds. Since then, puffin numbers have increased slightly and stabilised but today most Channel sites boast no more than a handful of birds. Burhou is an exception with some 300 puffins present each summer. The pattern of decline was repeated across the south, but this had little effect on the total population of the Atlantic puffin. Recent estimates suggest that there are around 15 million birds, the highest concentrations, over half, centred around Iceland, with big numbers in the north and west of Britain and northern Europe. In the Channel, they are at the extreme edge of their southern breeding range.

Puffins are members of the auk family, which includes guillemots and razorbills. Although small, standing little larger than a collared dove, puffins are easily recognised by their black and white plumage and, in summer, huge multi-coloured beak. Their appealing friendly dispositions and comical characteristics endear them to everyone. It is not until puffins are four or five years old that they display all the extravagant features of a fully mature bird. The bill of a year-old puffin is more angular and pointed, but with each passing year the colours become a little brighter, the markings a little more pronounced, and the size slowly increases. So too does the shape and colour of the 'make-up' surrounding the eye. Winter brings an apparent setback, as the puffin sheds the beak's decorative outer sheath, its face darkens and the ornamentation of the eyes disappear. Although the tip of the beak remains largely unchanged, its colour is dull, and its overall size looks a pale imitation of its summer splendour. Sightings of these drab little birds are rare, as they spend the winter months far out in the North Atlantic.

By mid-March, the first few puffins have returned after seven months away at sea, and are paddling around on the sheltered eastern side of Burhou. By the beginning of April, the colony is building and in fine weather the birds collect on the traditional rocks, close to the breeding slopes. Covered in the fine leaves of cliff spurrey with patches of bracken, the island has no trees to soften its hard edges, and great rocks bulge from the springy turf. In early summer broad areas of Burhou are coloured in a thick carpet of bluebells, looking strangely out of place. Even their colour is odd, a blue far deeper and of greater intensity than any found in the more familiar surrounds of a mainland deciduous wood. Walking on the island is not easy, as the turf is honeycombed in places with burrows. The extensive workings of rabbits and puffins have undermined large parts of the island. Storm petrels also nest underground, but being birds of the darkness they are seldom seen during the day. Puffins are more obvious, standing around on the island, floating in groups offshore or flying past in tight formation.

The wings of the puffin are a compromise between a means of flying and of propulsion underwater. The wing area is small in relation to body weight and so to maintain flight, the overloaded wings must flap frantically five or six beats per second. Gliding is almost impossible for these birds, except when riding the strong updrafts from cliffs, and becoming airborne from the sea is particularly hard work. The puffin scuttles across the surface, webbed feet racing over the water whilst wings whirr to take-off speed. It nearly always takes off into the wind, seeming to bounce off the waves, and in rough weather several attempts

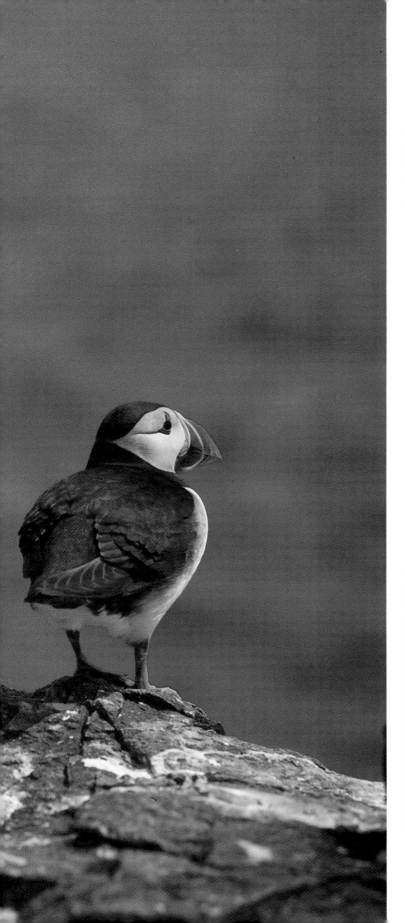

Left: *Puffins are gregarious birds, gathering together on outcrops of rock at the end of the day. Although some occur on other Channel Islands, their biggest and most important colony is on Burhou.*

Below: *The chicks of the great black-back gull. Its parents are the principal predators of puffins.*

may be needed. Once airborne, the bird flies low, within 1–2 metres of the surface, and is capable of achieving speeds of around 80 kilometres an hour. Landing is seldom elegant in a choppy sea or heavy swell. Puffins appear to simply lose height until they hit the first wave and pile into the next. On calm water the approach is more controlled, though equally lacking in grace. When touchdown is imminent the birds just stop flying and belly-flop into the sea. Upon landing a puffin nearly always plunges its head beneath the surface, presumably to check whether it has landed on any potential predators or supplies of fish. Whatever the reason, this and other antics never fail to amuse.

Puffins hide their real talent underwater. In the muted world of seawash and wave-patterned sun, the birds are truly at home, capable of diving to depths of 10 metres or more. The wings are used as paddles and the feet for changes in direction. However, to describe their aquatic movement as paddling would be an injustice, because underwater, puffins combine manoeuvrability and grace with an extraordinary turn of speed. Their agility is born of necessity, for their diet consists almost entirely of fast little fish. Although research reveals that they take some pelagic worms, a few molluscs, shrimps and other crustaceans, the birds feed their young mainly on sand eel, herring or sprat. An adult puffin requires some forty fish a day, depending on size, and so its diving skills have had to become pre-eminent, even at the expense of flight.

It is when a puffin is fishing that its extravagant bill can be seen to serve a serious and practical purpose. After dives lasting up to a minute, but usually less than half that time, the puffin may emerge juggling several fish in its beak. This feat requires hardware as well as skill. The bird attempts to catch the fish just behind the gills, although they can be manoeuvred in the beak with apparent ease. Indeed, a puffin can even swallow small fish underwater. The bird's beak has a strong vice-like grip and inward-facing serrations along its edge keep slippery meals in place. The upper and lower beak come together in parallel, so that equal pressure is applied from front to rear. Once a fish is caught and transferred to the back of the beak, it is held in place by the bird's powerful grooved tongue, which clamps it firmly to the roof, leaving the puffin free to pursue and catch more fish.

Several dives may be required before the beak is full and the bird sometimes maximises the available space by arranging the fish head to tail. The bird's preferred diet of long, thin fish can be more clearly seen when it returns to land. Standing briefly outside its burrow it peers nervously around, with its silvery cargo dangling either side of the beak. The reason for its choice of fish also becomes apparent. Many more long, thin fish can be carried in this way than short fat ones, and the chick presumably finds them easier to consume. During the process of catching and swallowing, puffins inevitably take in quantities of sea water. This is no problem for them because they share with other seabirds the remarkable ability to excrete excess salt through the kidneys and, even more efficiently, through special nasal glands.

Birds such as puffins that spend much of their lives in the sea must ensure that the cold salt water does not come in contact with their warm dry skin. Preening is therefore of paramount importance, and puffins spend around two hours each day just tending to their feathers. This both maintains the feathers in good condition for flight, and cleans, oils and arranges them back into an effective waterproof and insulating layer. However, the protective feathers do not last forever. As in most birds, the rigours of breeding tend to inflict the greatest damage on plumage. Eventually the feathers become very worn and soiled, and the birds then need to moult. Body feathers are lost gradually in order to maintain vital insulation. While the majority of birds also lose and replace flight feathers a few at a time over an extended period, auks and other water birds, such as swans, ducks and geese, shed all their flight feathers at once. During this fast moult the birds become flightless. But since the puffin's ability to fly would be seriously impaired by the loss of just one or two primary feathers, a less drastic measure would simply extend the danger. The rapid moult of the puffin usually takes place far out to sea between January and March, although first-year birds may moult a little later.

In new suits of feathers and wings in fine fettle, the fully mature birds are ready to breed. The main puffin colony is based around the turfed slopes in which the birds can burrow. Since they find difficulty in taking off from flat ground, they tend to colonise the steeper slopes first. Ideally, the area should also be bare of tall plant cover, giving an unobstructed view. Puffins appear nervous on land and seem to need the reassurance of others in view, especially the younger, less experienced birds. Fights over territory are not uncommon and some may last for up to a quarter of an hour and even continue in the sea. However, for much of the time the colony is a peaceful place full of activity.

For puffins, the main advantages of nesting in a colony are safety in numbers and the ease of finding a mate. There seems to be no real effort made to attract a partner. A puffin simply investigates a particular hole, and pairs up with one of the opposite sex that approves its choice. Bonding comes later, as the pair dig, rest and defend their burrow together. A pair may commandeer a surface rabbit hole, a powerful peck doubtless driving off any resident rabbits that are reluctant to leave. They are also more than capable of excavating their own

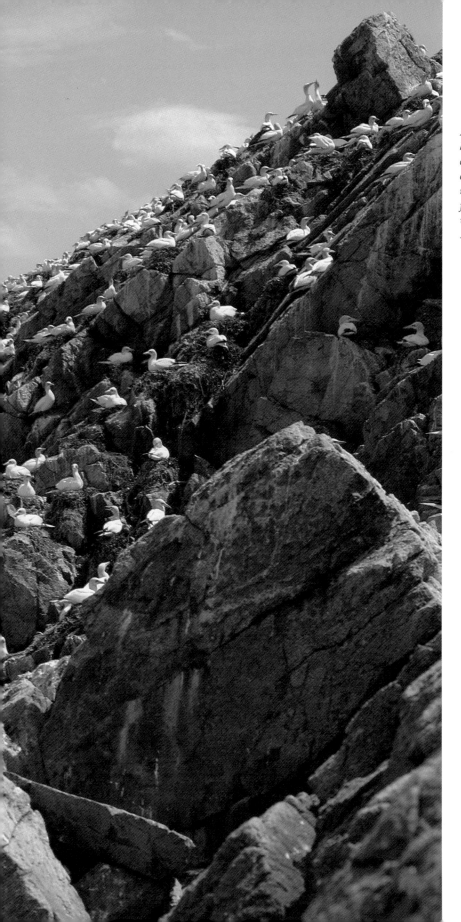

Amid the clamour of hundreds of gannets calling and the overpowering smell of rotting seaweed and fish, is a bird's-eye view of the Garden Rocks breeding colony.

burrow, one bird guarding the entrance while the other is down below digging. The puffin tears at the ground with its beak, and shuffles the soil back with its feet. Every so often the digger surfaces looking like a black-faced miner to shake its plumage clean. Once the burrow is complete, mutual billing and head flicking are the preludes to mating and laying.

The nesting chamber lies at the end of the burrow, and some females put great effort into collecting plants and feathers, which they scatter untidily around. Other puffins do not bother with nesting material at all. The first week of May is the peak time for laying, each female producing a single egg that is about the average size of a chicken's. In due course, its whiteness is discoloured by surface stains and soiling. Both parents incubate the egg, although the female seems to do most of the sitting, and after six weeks the puffin chick emerges into a dark and dingy world.

Wet and black at first, the young puffin soon dries into a bundle of fluff, brown-black with a pale underside. For the first few days it is closely brooded, and after that, the parents return at regular intervals with a load of fish to dump at its feet. The greatest activity takes place in the first few hours after dawn. By midday the colony is quiet, and small rafts of puffin float offshore. In the late afternoon, the rush begins again, as new supplies of fish are ferried to the burrows. At four weeks of age the chick is still covered in thick down, but this only serves to protect its growing adult feathers from being soiled underground. It has also attained its maximum weight, and from then on is fed less food and becomes increasingly restless. It wanders up and down the burrow, exercising and stretching wings and feet in a fitness routine that builds muscle at the expense of fat. It carefully avoids the entrance, preferring the dark recesses to the light, until it is about five weeks old, when the young puffin views the outside world for the first time.

Each evening, fly pasts of puffins bring whirring wings close to the cliff edge. The purpose of these is not clear but it is thought that squadrons of fast-moving birds are likely to confuse any predators. The principal threat on Burhou comes from the air, in the shape of the great black-backed gull. Dwarfing the auks in size, these massive birds have a wing span of well over 1.5 metres, making them the biggest gulls in the world. They are more than capable of taking adult puffins, let alone the chicks, and frequently do so. The sudden appearance of a great black-backed over a puffin colony usually causes panic. The puffins dive for their burrows or leap from the cliffs, while at sea the little birds scatter and duck underwater.

The five-week-old puffin chicks spend a few more days in relative safety underground, as they lose the soft downy covering worn since hatching. The down is shed in a sudden moult lasting only three or four days, to reveal the glossy black plumage of a young adult sitting amid the fluff-filled soil of the burrow. Parental attention then comes to an end and the chick is on its own. On a warm July night it appears at the burrow entrance, but does not stay there for long. As soon as darkness conceals and settles the nearby gulls, it leaves. Many chicks may depart on the same night. Scurrying and fluttering in unaccustomed urgency, they make their way down the slope, before tumbling over the cliff edge and falling into the sea. Having left the warm dry safety of the burrow just a few minutes before, they enter a new world, cold, wet and dangerous, as if born to it, as indeed they were. By the time dawn breaks over the coast of France and the pale light reveals the crying gulls wheeling overhead, the young puffins are already far out to sea.

The island of Burhou is protected by the States of Alderney as a nature reserve. It is closed during the breeding season so that the puffins can remain undisturbed in summer, and their tunnels safe from trampling. With such attractions, there may yet come a time when thousands of puffins return once again to crowd the island's slopes. Burhou is not the only jewel in Alderney's seabird crown. A few hundred metres off the precipitous south-west cliffs stand Les Etacs or the Garden Rocks, which grow white with gannets each summer. Another gannet colony lies to the west, between Burhou and the Casquets, on the massive rock dome of Ortac that rises 25 metres high. A gannet found nesting on its rugged top in 1940 provided the first record of this bird breeding anywhere in the Channel Islands. News then came of others found off northern Brittany, on Les Sept Îles. The Second World War had already begun and, within a few weeks of the nest being found, the people of Alderney were evacuated and the island left to the invading enemy forces. After liberation, in the summer of 1945, the inhabitants of Alderney began to return and discovered that the gannets had, meanwhile, also colonised the Garden Rocks. A year later the Garden Rocks' colony had grown to 200 pairs of gannets, and further west, Ortac had an expanded population of 250 pairs of birds. By 1968 the Alderney gannet colonies contained some 2000 pairs of breeding birds.

Today, gannet numbers have stabilised because their nests now occupy every available ledge and rocky outcrop. There is no better place in Europe to see a spectacular colony of gannets than amid the thrift and daisy-adorned turf on Alderney overlooking the Garden Rocks. This site looks impressive from the nearby cliffs of Trois Vaux Bay, but its scale can only really be appreciated when approaching by sea, carried along in a swirling tide towards sheer walls that

Below: *Gannets incubate a single, chalky white egg using the warmth from their big webbed feet.*

Right: *Sunset on Alderney is accompanied by the wind-drifted sounds of seabirds from the Garden Rocks, while beyond lies the other gannet colony of Ortac and the lonely Casquette lighthouse.*

rise abruptly to a height of nearly 40 metres. The strong currents tearing past this towering colony protect its occupants from intruders. However, gannets are big birds and appear fearless, even in the presence of people. They are remarkably tolerant, but a fearsome sharp beak can deliver a nasty stab wound to someone who gets too close, and they do not hesitate to strike at each other.

Nothing in the bird world compares with the overpowering presence and incessant roar of a thronging seabird city. At any time from the first few days of the new year, gannets are to be seen around the colony, and numbers increase until breeding gets underway in March. Each pair requires enough space for themselves, a large chick and a safe place for both taking-off and landing. Other factors which may decide the actual density of nest sites is unclear, but on suitable ground, the birds may just keep a beak's reach from each other. Living in such cramped quarters, the birds must signal their every intention lest a simple movement be taken as an act of aggression. Even the intention to take flight is indicated by a pointed beak reaching skyward before any attempt is made. In particular, pairs of gannets communicate with great ritual.

The more experienced males return to the colony first and proclaim ownership of a nest site by a bowing display, in which the bird dips its bill from side to side with its wings held out. A loud threatening call reinforces his position, but even so, fights are fierce and frequent. Once his site is established, he signals that he is looking for a mate. In this advertising display, he shakes his head vigorously from side to side while keeping his head low and wings closed. The females, meanwhile, are flying low over the colony. When a prospective mate lands, the male seizes her by the neck and, if she is interested, she turns away submissively, presenting her nape. The male may also adopt the so-called pelican posture, tucking his beak into his neck, perhaps as a gesture of appeasement.

Once old pairs are reunited and new partnerships forged, the male surrenders the site to the female by flying off and returning again and again. Later he begins to bring back beakfuls of nesting material. Then both take up the pelican posture and raise their closed wings, a performance that is repeated whenever they are together at the site. These birds are silent away from the nest, but more than make up for it at home. At every stage during breeding, the adults exchange greetings when they meet up at the nest. The returning bird flies in, calling, and the mate responds by head shaking. He often gives her neck a nibble and she turns away. Then, standing breast to breast, they engage in mutual bill fencing, calling all the while.

The nest itself is a pile of seaweed and other flotsam collected offshore or pinched from nearby. Any nest left unattended for long is likely to shrink in size. From mid-April onwards, the female lays a single large white egg. The birds often take turns at incubation, which they do differently from the majority of other birds. Most parent birds pass their body heat to the eggs through an area of bare skin on the breast known as a brood patch. Gannets, however, are well covered with feathers and so warm the eggs using their large, webbed feet, which they place carefully over the egg before settling down. The young are most vulnerable to the cold when soaked by rain, and in rough weather the parents sit very tight. Although keeping up the temperature is important on cold days, heat is a much quicker killer of eggs. In the blazing sun, gannets can be seen just shading the nest, their bright white feathers reflecting the burning rays. They dissipate their own heat by panting, with beak open and the throat expanded and fluttered. The chick, which hatches after some forty-four days, also keeps cool in this way. Their mess may help too, because the white guano-splashed rocks probably reflect much of the sun's heat. Nesting in such large visible colonies they have no need to keep their excreta from marking the site.

Gannets catch food in spectacular fashion, sometimes from a considerable height above the sea. They dive headlong, wings folded back at the last second, and plunge like a white missile through the surface. Mackerel are their favourite fish and flocks of gannets gather over large shoals, diving and surfacing, taking off and plunging again beneath the waves. When a parent returns to the nest, the youngster jumps headfirst into its gullet and gorges on the fish there. The young birds spend up to ninety days in the nest gaining weight and full-sized feathers. Then the juveniles must fly straight from their lofty sites, out to sea. The fortunate ones just jump and the instinct of flight takes over. Those born deeper into the colony must blunder their way through a lethal jungle of jostling birds and sharp beaks to find a suitable edge. Many of the immature gannets, mottled grey-brown in colour, migrate down to the tropical Atlantic off the coast of west Africa. They take three to four years before gaining the dazzling white body, buff-burnished head and jet-black wingtips of an adult. Only then will they return to breed.

By summer's end, the seabird sanctuaries are deserted, and the roar of gannets no longer echoes from the cliffs, nor does the screeching of terns fill the sky. Flowers fade on the tern tower, Burhou is left to the gulls and the Garden Rocks are enveloped in the hushed silence of the sea. But it is only a temporary lull for the many other plants and animals that permanently inhabit this unique part of Britain, a brief respite before the teeming hordes return.

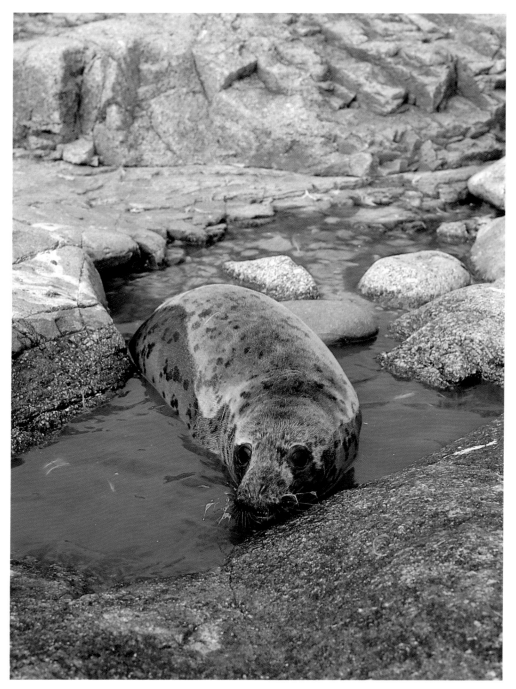

Born on one of the rugged Western Rocks several weeks ago, this young grey Atlantic seal has found a pool in which to wallow. Now, left on its own, hunger will eventually drive it to sea.

CHAPTER SIX

The Isles of Scilly

On A REMOTE rocky island in October, a seal pup lies alone among the boulders surrounded by its newly shed hair, its large eyes like pools of black liquid glinting in the gathering gloom. For this young grey Atlantic seal, finally deserted by its mother, it is a race against time to complete its first moult so that it can leave the island before the autumn gales begin. A full year will pass before its mother returns once again to breed and several more before the pup itself may come back to the place of its birth. These desolate islets and reefs where the seals come to breed are part of the Isles of Scilly, the formidable Western Rocks, scene of many shipwrecks over the centuries, lying at the extreme western approach to the English Channel.

Although situated only 43 kilometres south-west of Land's End, the Isles of Scilly are the most isolated inhabited islands in Britain. Separated from the mainland for many thousands of years and now lying scattered in the vastness of the Atlantic Ocean, their remoteness is highlighted by the fact that they are one of the few locations in Britain where the sun both rises and sets at sea.

Today, there are five inhabited islands: St Mary's, Tresco, St Martin's, Bryher and St Agnes, forty smaller islands with vegetation and some 150 named rocks. The flat-topped granite summits that make up the islands are divided by a shallow sea, for the whole archipelago is set on a submarine shelf that rises steeply from the sea floor some 80 metres below. So shallow is the sea that a fall in sea level of less than 10 metres would reunite most of the main group into a single land mass, as they once were in the past. A further drop of 10 metres would join St Agnes and the Western Rocks to the rest.

By far the biggest island in Scilly is St Mary's, but even that is small. If you could walk across the widest point in a straight line, it would take less than an hour. Even following the narrow roads and rutted lanes from Peninnis Head to Halangy Down does not take much longer. On a fine day, the view from Halangy Down – at 52 metres the islands' highest point – across the calm blue waters of the Sound looks like a white-beached archipelago set in a sub-tropical sea.

The islands are officially designated as an area of outstanding natural beauty and a conservation area, and the shoreline is a heritage coast. There are also twenty-three sites of special scientific interest, which together cover over half the land area. But titles alone cannot describe the islands' special quality. When compared to the mainland, the number of native plants on Scilly is small, as might be expected on remote Atlantic isles. But away from cultivated parts, where the islands are dominated by heather, gorse, bracken and brambles, a closer investigation reveals a treasure trove of plant life – many rare and endangered species thrive here.

The climate of Britain is heavily influenced by the Atlantic Ocean and the Isles of Scilly are at the extreme leading edge. Rainfall is regular though not always adequate, frosts are rare and snow is a notable event. Like all islands in European waters they have their fair share of strong winds and days of thick sea fog. Although humid, the air is enviably pure with a lack of airborne dust or pollution. The islands' sunshine record is almost the highest recorded in Britain but summer temperatures seldom rise too high for comfort. Winter is actually one of the busiest times for the islands' flower industry, with millions of early-year blooms being exported to mainland markets. Much of the inland area of the largest islands is used for growing bulbs and divided into small fields by shelter belts of trees and tall shrubs. The hedgerows, composed of exotic evergreens such as escallonia, pittosporum and veronica, are a relatively new feature which transformed the look of the islands at the end of the nineteenth century although 28 km were wiped out in 1987 by one week of frost and snow.

In the first week of March, while the rest of Britain still shivers in the last throes of winter, spring has already arrived on the Isles of Scilly. As the last of the winter crop of narcissus are cut, the first wild flowers spread a blaze of colour across the field. Over the years the bulb fields have developed their own unique flora, distinguished by species that grow throughout the coldest months.

One of the greatest discoveries for the cut-flower industry was that burning the bulb fields produces some earlier blooms. Scorching the ground three times during the summer also has an effect on the weeds, for while controlling many of the more common plants it allows the winter-growing varieties to flourish between the rows of cultivated bulbs. It is a fragile balance created by generations of farmers, but one which could so easily be destroyed if modern chemicals were used more extensively. Destruction of this balance would spell disappointment for many visitors to the islands who come early in the year to marvel at the spectacle of colour as soleil d'or, Scilly whites and daffodils give way to wild flowers. The fields start to blaze again with yellow, but this time there are Bermuda buttercups mixed with a rare western fumitory, pink oxalis, speedwell and prickly fruited buttercup. Tiny catchfly flowers, rosy garlic and Babbington leek also bloom as the weeks pass. And as these exotic flowers from as far away as South Africa, America and the Mediterranean set seed, a new flush of colour spreads. Whistling jacks and Spanish iris, former crops now growing wild, add to the succession of flowers in vibrant display, appearing between the winter daffodils and summer corn marigold.

The islands have few freshwater streams and no natural tree cover, although there is evidence that woodland existed in prehistoric times. Today, the only woods of any size are the planted Abbey Woods on Tresco and a grove of fine elms on the Garrison and at the Holy Vale on St Mary's. Since the ravages of Dutch elm disease on the mainland, this is now one of the few places in Britain where it is possible to walk beneath the leafy boughs of mature elm trees.

Open freshwater pools are also uncommon on islands so heavily influenced by the sea, and some would be better described as brackish rather than pure. The island of Bryher has two on the west coast that are very different in character. The salt-sprayed waters of Great Pool are thick with pondweed and sea milkwort, and surrounded by saltmarsh rush. In contrast, the fresher Little Pool supports an abundance of crowfoot and marshwort, which are less tolerant of salt. The Big Pool on St Agnes also has sea clubrush. Tresco's Abbey Pool is more sheltered. This is reflected in the wealth of its flora and its rich muddy margins which are so attractive to birdlife. On St Mary's, Porthellick Pool is closer to the sea, separated only by a shingle ridge. On its sea side are plants that are able to endure a high level of salt, such as sea rush, scentless mayweed and yellow horned poppy. Further from the sea the decreasing salinity is revealed by the spread of greater reedmace, and stands of lesser spearwort, hemlock water dropwort and yellow flag iris. Inland, more impressive than colourful, stand tall stacks of tussock sedge and elegant royal ferns.

If you climb to the exposed heights of the larger islands, where the soil lies thinly over the granite, the ground is dominated by ling. For most people this plant is just another heather, with pale purple flower spikes. But on this wind-beaten terrain it is very special. The headlands of Bryher and St Martin's, and Castle Down, Tresco, are maritime heaths of great proportion, open to the full force of Atlantic gales. Battered and beaten by howling winds and splattered by salt, the ling grows short, gnarled and knotted, the plants bending permanently away from the prevailing winds in a series of undulating ridges and troughs. To walk across the waves of this heathland landscape is to journey back in time. It is thought that possibly at one time, vast stretches of the

Above, top: *Bermuda buttercups and western fumitory are common and colourful weeds of the islands' bulb fields.*

Above: *Flowers and fishing play an important part in the life of the Isles of Scilly.*

Right: *The fractured and faulted granite headlands of the island's exposed coast are smoothed and worn into fantastic shapes by the sea.*

exposed cliff tops of western Europe may have looked very much like this.

By July, the ubiquitous bracken smothers all but the smallest islands. In some sheltered places its height is phenomenal, greater than a person. But before its rapid growth blankets the slopes, the ground is carpeted with bluebells. The presence of these plants is an unexpected pleasure, for how do they manage to survive? It is difficult to equate their windswept island home with the tranquillity of a mainland bluebell wood, yet the habitats do have features in common. A lack of competition from more vigorous plants and high humidity is combined with the most important factor of all, deep shade in summer to protect them from the sun's rays. The early flowering bluebell plants thrive equally well beneath either a protective canopy of tree leaves or the fronds of the islands' bracken.

Scilly has only a few places where granite cliffs drop steeply into the sea. More than half the coastline of the islands is made up of low cliffs crumbling on to a narrow foreshore, where boulder heaps litter the shingle and stretches of sand. The rock-strewn ground only supports plants tolerant of parched, salty conditions, and most of those growing here have thick fleshy water-storing leaves. Sea beet is commonly found with scurvy grass, bittersweet and daisy-flowered sea mayweed. Further up the shore grow pockets of rock samphire and spurrey, while drifts of sea pinks colour the higher shore. Tree mallow is common but its Cretan relative is confined to the mild south-west, and both grow on Scilly. More invasive is the South African fig which now covers many cliffs along the Channel shores. On Scilly, as elsewhere, its spread has been facilitated by gulls. And on islands where suitable nesting material is scarce the fig can be found cascading down over rocks, emanating from the nests of herring gulls. The plant is quite capable of taking root from a single fleshy leaf.

There are some plants, however, that have a far longer history on Scilly, and an importance out of all proportion to their size. Hiding in the close-cropped turf is a tiny flower, the orange birdsfoot trefoil, which is unknown on the British mainland. This relic species grew here before the last ice age when the climate was much warmer, and still survives. Only a little bigger is the attractive dwarf pansy. Found more commonly in southern Europe, it is at the very northern edge of its range here.

The inexorable erosion of the granite has produced great quantities of white quartz sand, which spreads across the floor of the shallow sea, dividing the islands and forming their dazzling beaches. These beaches, often backed by dunes, extend along as much as a quarter of the coastline. Even at the height of the summer season it is possible to walk a wave-lapped shore without finding another human footprint. On the clean white sand the nutrients lost by the winter stranding of seaweeds are gained by other plants. Sea purslane and rocket, as well as prickly saltwort grow just beyond the reach of high tide. Higher up the gently sloping shore the growth of sand sedge and marram grass begins the process of stabilising the sand, trapping the wind-blown grains and allowing the blue thistle-like sea holly and the yellow horned poppy to take root.

Over the centuries, storm-driven sand has blown inshore forming dunes and bars that link some of the islands, and in a few places sand is actually raising the height of the land. The finest examples of dunes are found on the three largest islands. In Scilly, however, nothing is quite the same as elsewhere, and the dunes support a striking flora. Primroses sprouting from sand sheltering between the sharp marram stems look out of place. More natural are the deep yellow splashes of birdsfoot trefoil along with sea storksbill, Portland and sea spurge. But the way these dunes differ from all others is best seen on Tresco after mid-summer. Then glorious blue flower-heads standing clear of the grass give the dunes a decidedly exotic look. Agapanthus, a native flower of South Africa introduced to Tresco in the nearby Abbey gardens, has become widely established and now thrives in the wild.

All doubts about the island's claim of having a climate so mild that it borders on the sub-tropical are dispelled by a stroll through the world-famous Abbey gardens. In 1834 when Tresco was a windswept, treeless isle, Augustus Smith built his home and gardens in the lee of high walls and a shelter belt of trees and foreign shrubs. Today, beneath towering date palms, pink *Proteas* from South Africa and huge flame trees from New Zealand, grow giant *Echiums* and Bird of Paradise flowers. Plants from all over the world survive in the open, as nowhere else in Europe. Even the native birds now have a taste for the exotic. The tall *Puya* plants from the Andes in Chile produce copious quantities of nectar, which attract an abundance of ants and other insects. In their homeland the amazing jade-green waxy flowers are pollinated by the heads of nectar-seeking birds. In Scilly that job is performed by blackbirds and starlings delving into the blooms, but as well as sipping the nectar it seems that some are more interested in searching for the insects. So the Tresco birds get a sugar-dipped, protein-filled snack and the plants are cross-pollinated. So profuse is the pollen production at times that many birds wear a bright yellow 'cap' in season. In dry weather some birds have also learnt to visit the garden plants after a shower of rain. A few large flowers retain some water and the birds eagerly quench their thirst from the ready-sweetened cups. Sparrows, too, get in on the act but the reputation of these birds is more that of vandals. Although they can commonly

Right: *Big Pool on St Agnes is the most south-westerly freshwater to be found in Britain. An important place for migrant birds.*

Below: *The colourful swathes of sea thrift on Annet are one of the best examples of such maritime turf in the British Isles.*

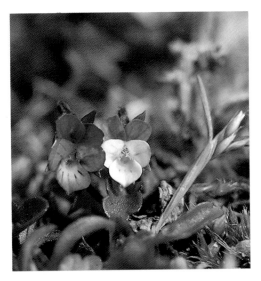

Left: The tiny dwarf pansy is an island speciality. Unknown on the British mainland, it is a southern European plant.

Below: The common birdsfoot trefoil gives a splash of colour to the dunes and coastal heathlands in mid-summer. The name refers to its long curling seed pods.

be seen just sipping nectar, their short beaks do not allow them to probe deep into long-tubed flowers so they simply rip the blooms apart.

The number of plant and animal species introduced to the island, whether deliberately or accidentally, have added to the variety of life. But some are more welcome than others. Among the antipodean stowaways arriving from the other side of the earth came two species of flatworm and a lively amphipod akin to the native sandhopper. Whereas the native species of hopper is confined to the shore, the New Zealand hopper has taken to life on land in a big way. These little animals are now to be found on most main islands, shunning light, hiding beneath rocks and stones, scattering in jumping masses if disturbed.

The Abbey gardens hide another stranger to these islands but one that lurks among the bushes and is a master of disguise. Stick insects are aptly named. Precisely where they came from and when is still not known, but they were discovered here in the 1960s and it is assumed they were introduced along with many plants from New Zealand. Two species, the prickly and the smooth, were found and both seemed to be thriving until the unusually cold winter of 1987. Then at the end of 1989 and the start of 1990 near-hurricane force winds devastated many of the island's trees and the gardens were badly hit. Shelter belts and tall plants were blown flat or torn from the ground. As in other areas where the storm struck the Abbey gardens are recovering and although the numbers of stick insects are much diminished, they still survive.

Living twigs are easily overlooked, but not all island insects lead such a sheltered existence. In 1940, a large species of ant was identified close to one of the landing places on St Martin's. Known in Britain only from one other small site in south-east England, it was at first thought to have been accidentally introduced. The ant is unlikely to have made the long sea crossing on its own, as it has limited powers of flight. Subsequent searches failed to find any more until, in 1967, several colonies were discovered on the headlands and the adjacent Eastern Isles. It has been suggested that, like the tiny-flowered trefoil, this population of ants may even be a relic from warmer times and was simply not recognised earlier.

Big beetles are much easier to see and few are more obvious than the brilliant green rose chafer. An appetite for petals makes this relative of the scarab beetle forage on the cliffs. On a warm summer's day the sound of the beetles' whirring flight can fill the air as they search for the large white landing pads that are the flowers of the wild carrot, one of their favourite foods. Common on the islands, they are harmless although, like many beetles, their larvae feed on roots. The brilliant colouring of this chafer is in marked contrast to a black variety which also thrives here. Apart from colour the beetles appear identical, but the dark relation is only found elsewhere in the Channel Islands and on Corsica in the Mediterranean.

More formidable looking, but equally harmless as far as people are concerned, is the large black slow-crawling oil-beetle, so named from its habit of producing an unpleasant fluid when repelling predators. In spring the female beetle lays several hundred eggs that hatch into extremely active minute yellow creatures with long legs and bristles. These swarm over the grass and flowers, climbing upwards at every opportunity, as their lives depend on the chance of meeting a bee. To survive, the oil-beetle's offspring must hitch a lift back to the bee's nest where they raid one of the bee nursery cells and gorge themselves on the eggs. Afterwards they undergo a complex change and then take over the food store intended for the bee larvae. In their frantic scramble to board a passing bee, the oil-beetle's offspring seem unable to sense whether they have chosen the right lift. Consequently their lives are often brought to a premature end by hitching a lift with a fly or other flying insect, so the fecundity of the oil-beetle is offset by the inevitable death of many offspring.

The soft sandy strata of some of Scilly's low cliffs are ideal excavation sites for mining bees. Andrena bees are a group of solitary bees containing some sixty different species. The species found on Scilly is small and dark coloured, and as in most species of mining bee the female digs a tunnel alone, making perhaps six or so earthen chambers in which to lay eggs. There is no parental care. The female shows no interest in the burrow after she has finished constructing it and laid in provisions for her brood. Although solitary, the individual nests are often so closely packed together that they appear to be a thriving colony, yet each maintains its separate life. Despite being common in Scilly this mining bee is another mainland rarity.

Unlike mining bees, bumble bees are sociable. But British colonies are not big; even the largest nests seldom contain more than 400 individuals and most are much smaller. The majority of nests are situated underground in a warm dry place. Only one species thrives in damp conditions and that is the moss carder bees, which build their homes in marsh and coastal areas, often above ground and deep in moss. These bees have attractive, orange-brown and yellow colouring, and some island races are distinctively marked. A bumble bee has a heavy body and therefore has comparatively broad wings to produce the lift it requires to get airborne. Beating needs considerable strength and the bee's thorax is crammed with muscles but, like most engines, warmth is required for them to work at full power and provide the energy needed to lift the plump

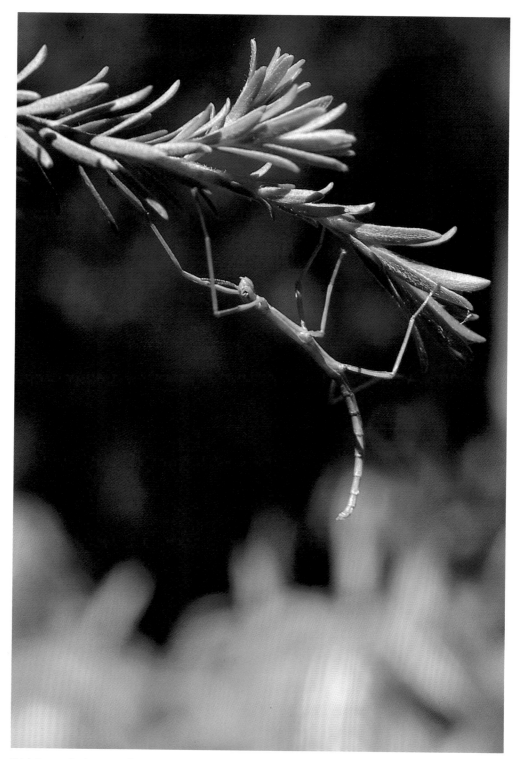

Stick insects lurk among the exotic vegetation found in the shelter of the Abbey Gardens on Tresco. Their numbers were much reduced by the unusually cold winter of 1987.

little body into the air. Unlike birds, bees and other insects cannot maintain the heat in their bodies overnight. Their warmth must come from the sun. But bees, even on chilly mornings, are capable of making a cold start. They shiver just as we do to warm our muscles. The wings are vibrated until the temperature of the body is warm enough for flying. In order to retain this warmth bees have a covering of hair which helps to reduce the heat loss. Dampness combined with cold is a lethal combination for bees, hence their need for a dry nest. Moss carder bees, however, seem to cope with the damp conditions, but then they are limited in their range. Like other bumble bees all moss carders die at the onset of winter except new queens, which survive to form a new colony the following year. They begin to appear in the early spring, visiting some of the islands' seasonal specialities, flowers such as the white bells of the three-cornered leek. But this moss carder is no ordinary bee, it is a distinct subspecies, an island race that only otherwise occurs on Alderney in the Channel Islands. When I first found this particular bee in 1980, its name was known only to science. It seemed obvious to give *Bombus muscorum scyllionus* a common name, so I did – the Scilly bee.

Many of the uninhabited isles are closed to people during the summer season. One such is Tean, a tiny haven of tranquillity in Scilly's shallow sea. So small is it, that its entire length could be walked in only 15 minutes, although, like many of these sheltered islands, some parts are covered by an impenetrable jungle of bracken and bramble. Tean first became the focus of attention in 1938, when a butterfly was discovered that differed from others of its kind. Tean's common blue is anything but common. Incredibly, the normal form of the butterfly is found on the three largest islands, including St Martin's, which at one point is only 300 metres away. Subtle changes in the pattern of spots and colour have occurred in isolation, giving the wings an extensive scattering of pale silvery-blue scales. Common blue butterflies rarely stray far from their place of hatching, so variations tend to be highly localised. Perhaps this is the first stage in the evolution of a new subspecies. Another butterfly found on Scilly has already taken this step. The meadow brown is a clumsy flier, seldom travelling far and well known for its regional varieties. On Scilly the meadow brown is unique. Colour and size are the main considerations, but the pattern and distribution of black spots on the underside of the wing are the markers that measure the separate island races. On Tean alone there appear to be three distinct types, each displaying a different number of spots. Remarkably, the populations live on three different hills, just a stone's throw apart.

The Isles of Scilly are home to only about one-quarter of the butterflies found

Left: *The formidable natural rock fortress of Men-a-Vaur is an important seabird sanctuary.* **Above:** *The Scilly bee is a distinct sub-species found only on the Isles of Scilly and on the Channel Island of Alderney.*

Right: *The black variety of the green rose chafer is only encountered elsewhere across the Channel or in the Mediterranean.* **Below:** *This young sandwich tern survived the summer gale by seeking shelter on its islet home.*

in Britain. This is hardly surprising considering their geographical location. As in all animal populations, people included, there are residents, regular visitors and various passage species, which make brief but welcome appearances on the islands. The native butterflies of Scilly include the common blue, meadow brown, speckled wood, peacock and small tortoiseshell. Of the visiting migrants that show up annually, painted ladies and red admirals frequent the same places year after year, enjoying the sunshine. But the real rarities, such as monarch butterflies, cause quite a stir. The monarch or milkweed butterfly from North America is a well-known long-distance traveller. Occasionally, perhaps blown off course, some manage a transatlantic crossing. In 1968, over fifty monarch butterflies were recorded from the south-west of England, and individuals can appear in any year. Another migrant, but one from southern Europe, becomes almost common in hot summers. This is the clouded yellow, which may be seen tirelessly beating its way along the back of the shore and patrolling hedgerows and banks.

Terrestrial life, it seems, becomes increasingly precarious the smaller the area of land on which it lives. While migrants come and go, residents must be able to survive all year. This can be seen time and again when looking at island species – the largest islands have most animal life, the smallest rocks none at all. Scilly has no reptiles, except for a few pet slow-worms that gave their owners the slip. And there is only one species of amphibian – frogs are common on St Mary's.

Central to the Isles of Scilly is the shallow water of Crow Sound. This is so shallow in parts that it is possible to walk the sands between many of the islands at the lowest spring tide. The sea around Scilly is cool and sparkling clear. The absence of rivers transporting mud or industrial effluents gives these waters a clarity that draws scuba divers from all over the world. Now the entire offshore area, down to the 50-metre contour, has been declared a marine park to protect and conserve it. This remarkable environment encompasses a seascape of extremes, from gentle flats, where the sand is so fine and waters so calm that beds of eel grass grow, to the incredible rugged world of the Western Rocks. A new classification of shore type was added to the British list specially for Scilly. To describe the scale of underwater chasms and sheer walls, sharp reefs and wave-smashed ledges needed a new title: 'super-exposed'. What is even more extraordinary is the ability of living organisms to survive such appalling conditions. Yet they do. Long-lived and slow-growing, sea fans and corals cling extravagantly to the rocks. But even in these turbulent waters, perhaps the greatest danger they face is still from people.

Wading in the water on the lee of an island on a calm day it is another world, where the biggest waves are the ripples made by splashing feet. The ebb of the crystal clear water at low tide reveals a fascinating shore. Many common mainland species are absent or rare and others not normally found in Britain are abundant. It is a pattern repeated at all levels, both on land and at sea. In the coarser gravels giant top-shells, tube-dwelling parchment worms and a burrowing anemone are notable rarities. There are also four types of marine algae of national importance. Montague's blenny, which is only very occasionally found along the south coast of England, is the most common fish of rock pools. More extraordinary still are the creatures that normally live in much deeper water. The rose feather star uses its delicate arms not only for catching plankton, but also for swimming. Its stroke is a slow undulating motion, little changed over millions of years from a time when creatures just like it paddled through prehistoric seas. In Scilly it is also found between the tides. Even humble hermit crabs merit a second glance. In 1962, a species new to Britain was discovered hiding in a shell, waving its brilliant violet antennae. It was previously only known around Mediterranean shores and up the Atlantic coast as far as Brittany.

The islands support few resident birds compared with similar habitats on the mainland. It is interesting to note that there are no woodland birds except for blue tits and great tits on Tresco and St Mary's. But Scilly has a thriving population of skylarks and linnets, and thrushes, blackbirds, starlings, wrens, robins, chaffinches and sparrows are all common. All these have taken to island life so well that many can often be found down on the shore. It is not unusual to see a robin foraging in the seaweed or a songthrush hammering snails on a boulder lapped by waves. The sight of such birds hopping along a beach on the mainland would look decidedly odd, but here it is a simple adaptation enabling them to profit from a limited terrain. The birds are also very tame, especially on Tresco. This is thought to be due to the lack of ground predators and the scarcity of aerial predators. Although crows and birds of prey are occasionally seen, only kestrels are commonly resident, so small birds have less reason to be wary.

As with many isolated communities there are species that reveal their insular lives in subtle ways. Wrens do not travel far and the island birds could perhaps be considered a separate race as they differ in many ways from the average wren. Their plumage is more rusty in colour, the line above the eye is brighter and their boldness is a marked contrast to the furtive behaviour of their mainland relative. Just as common are rock pipits. So, too, are cuckoos. This is no

Left: *Kittiwakes typically breed high on the most precipitous seacliffs, where they glue their nests of seaweed and mud to the narrowest ledges.*

Below: *The kittiwakes nesting on St Helens are an overspill from the nearby main colony on Men-a-Vaur. Round Island lighthouse lies beyond.*

coincidence for nine out of ten cuckoos born on the Isle of Scilly are hatched in rock pipit nests. Nesting migrants make up the largest part of the islands' breeding birds. Many more migrant birds do not stay to breed, but just stop off to replenish their food reserves. Others, blown off course, end up foraging on the shores: hoopoe, golden oriole and even bee-eaters appear from year to year. As an international avian airport Scilly takes some beating. Dropping in from North America, Asia and the Far East come more long-distance travellers. Buff-breasted sandpipers have turned up appropriately on the short grass of St Mary's airport, while another American bird, the red-eyed vireo, appears more frequently. Islands certainly seem to attract these rare vagrants, but perhaps not much more than the mainland. It is just that in the Scilly season for migrant birds, there are hundreds of high-powered telescopes and binoculars being focused by an influx of bird watchers, who are not only able to tell an Isabelline shrike from a Pallas's warbler, but can actually identify them.

In an average year fifty to sixty species of birds nest on the islands. The majority, not surprisingly, are seabirds. Some of the most beautiful are the terns: common, sandwich and rare roseate terns all nest here at times. But terns are fickle. Their choice of nesting colonies can vary from one year to the next. If the success of a species can be measured in terms of the expansion and contraction of its range, then the fortunes of birds breeding on the outermost edge of the range will register the greatest change. That probably applies as much to auks as it does to terns in the south of Britain, especially species such as the roseate. Scilly must be one of the last remaining southerly sites in Britain where these handsome birds still breed.

Sandwich terns sometimes breed within the colonies of more aggressive birds, presumably relying on their neighbours' defensive mobbing to drive away any intruders. In other areas sandwich tern colonies are associated with black-headed gulls, common terns and even the notorious great black-headed gulls. But in Scilly they tend to breed on the rocky islets lying in the shelter of larger islands. In some years, however, it is the weather rather than predation that takes the highest toll. Terns lay only one or two eggs and the young that hatch after about twenty-three days often form protective crèches, keeping close together in the shelter of the rocks. The most exposed of these islets are unfortunately at the mercy of the weather, and the birds are highly sensitive to disturbance just before and during incubation. One year a colony was safely established on one islet and twenty to thirty young were thought to have hatched. In the following week gale-force winds struck Scilly and persisted for two days and nights. A visit to the tern colony in the ensuing calm revealed a scene of utter devastation. Seaweed lay strewn across the rocks, partly covering many broken and gull-pecked eggs, and the pathetic, sodden remains of several young birds littered the summit. Not far away, less than a minute by air, lay another rocky islet, more sheltered and taller than the other. Here, terns were still calling overhead, while others returned with beakfuls of sand eels to be greeted by screaming young. Such is the lottery of nature that a few hundred metres separated failure and success.

Seabirds tend to select the most inhospitable places as nest sites. Few locations are more menacing than the towering dark shape of Menavaur, rising straight from the seabed on the exposed northern edge of the archipelago. Its three giant rock stacks are separated by two deep gullies which funnel the Atlantic swell. Waves enter, gathering height and fury between the converging walls before bursting through in an explosion of white water. Menavaur is the most impressive of all the islands' seabird sanctuaries. Guillemots crowd the rocks, while puffins nest among its crags. Razorbills, another member of the auk family, are even more numerous. Razorbills prefer the wild remoteness of island life to the high-rise cliffs of mainland coasts. Their colonies are usually found in the vicinity of the closely related guillemot, but razorbills keep to different parts of the cliff, laying a single egg in a sheltered cavity or beneath a rock towards the cliff top. Like all members of their clan they are expert swimmers and divers, pursuing similar prey to guillemots and puffins. Fulmars, too, breed on Menavaur and can be seen wheeling in the Atlantic winds. The noisiest residents, drowning the sound of the crashing waves with their cries, are the kittiwakes, which nest on the narrow ledges of the steep gully walls. Unlike other gulls, these attractive birds rarely fly inland to look for food, preferring to keep to the coasts for breeding and to feed offshore. On their transoceanic flights they live mainly on a diet of fish and fish remains, picked from the surface of the sea.

Kittiwakes generally choose the steepest cliffs with the narrowest of ledges for their nests. They are the only gulls to have mastered a technique for securing their nests to the rock. First they collect mud and deposit it on the chosen ledge. Using their black, webbed feet, they trample this down to form a firm base. Then moss, grass and seaweed are trodden into the mess and as it dries a solid cup takes shape. Sometimes kittiwakes are a little too enthusiastic at this stage and problems result: the most common cause of breeding failure is a fallen nest. Two or three eggs are laid in the completed nest and incubated for up to a month. After hatching the young remain in the nest for more than six weeks. They quickly develop long, sharp claws that enable them to cling on safely. In keeping

Above left: *The lesser black-backed gull is common in the islands, nesting on the ground in large noisy colonies.*

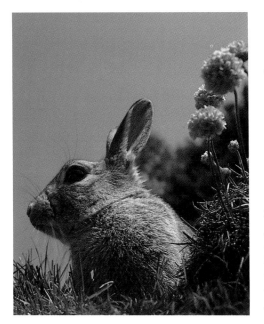

Left: *The earliest record of the rabbit in Britain comes from Scilly. They are today found on most of the islands.*

Below left: *Manx shearwater only come ashore to breed, and then only under the cover of darkness.*

Below: *South-west from the boulder shores of Annet lie the notorious Western Rocks, a hazard to shipping but a haven for seabirds and seals.*

with their precarious position the chicks' antics are subdued and they usually keep well down in the nest. When an adult returns with food the young do not launch themselves in a screaming mob as many chicks do, mugging the parent for food. They solicit carefully and are fed in turn, directly from the parent's throat. Presumably there is less chance of a fatal slip in a well-behaved family.

Even when they start to exercise their wings young kittiwakes maintain a tight grip on the nest. As the time to leave the nest approaches the young seem to undergo a fundamental change. Having spent the first twenty-eight days or so of their life clinging to the nest, crouching low and gripping tight for hours on end in the face of howling gales, the juvenile birds seem unable to readily reverse this instinctive behaviour. The process of preparing themselves for the biggest leap of their life is almost visible and several hours may elapse during which the parents' calls to their young rise to a crescendo in the air. Then, while the adults continue to call, the juvenile birds begin to collect on a nearby rock, feeding, flying, resting and watching the antics of the colony.

It seems that nesting in a colony is a powerful social stimulus that ensures synchronisation. First-time breeders benefit from the older birds' lead, and the younger ones on the less sought-after sites, tend to suffer the highest mortality. As far as most seabirds are concerned, breeding seems to be limited by the availability of sites. New colonies sometimes appear quite close to existing ones. St Helen's, an island adjacent to Menavaur, has a thriving overspill colony of kittiwakes nesting in a cliff gully.

Puffins are affectionately known locally as Scilly parrots. The earliest record of the puffin comes from a reference to the Isles of Scilly in AD 1337 and shows both how highly valued and how numerous the birds were in the past. When the Black Prince was made Duke of Cornwall in that year, the islands were listed under foreign rents, the payment being 300 puffins. Their numbers are much reduced nowadays, but for the past decade their population has remained stable at around 100 pairs. Scilly puffins appear to be more wary than those found elsewhere and are almost secretive in habit, nesting in deep burrows excavated between rocks or under overhanging cliffs rather than on accessible slopes. Small colonies carry a consequently higher risk of predation and here, great black-backed gulls and scavenging rats are the puffins' enemies.

The biggest colony of puffins lies beyond St Agnes, on the more exposed western isle of Annet. Annet is an uninhabited nature reserve of unique beauty and importance. Long and low, it is spectacular early in the season when the sea pink or thrift is in full bloom. This is one of the best displays of these maritime flowers to be found anywhere in the British Isles with huge clumps, several metres in width, rising in pink-tinged domes. The colour of the flowers varies widely from some that are deep rose-pink to others that are barely suffused with a blush and are nearly white. Hidden between the hummocks are a few nests of the great black-backed gulls. While one bird sits on the eggs, its mate stands on nearby rocks watching other seabirds for the chance of a meal.

The other end of the island is a complete contrast. The vegetation is scant and the scene is dominated by the commotion of a scattered colony of birds. Nesting neatly spaced on the ground are lesser black-backed gulls. Their numbers far exceed those of their great relatives nesting among the thrift and they, too, are scavengers. Along with the herring gull, they have a taste for carrion and readily thieve unattended nests. Although lesser black-backed gulls are migrants, they have shown an increasing tendency to overwinter around the British coast. Opportunist birds, they will take urban refuse if given the chance. Here, in summer, they spend much of their time plunge-diving into the waves just offshore and, with a predilection for taking fish and other creatures washed on to rocks and beaches, they find plenty of pickings in the turbulent waters of these isles.

On Annet, the best is hidden until last. On a summer evening, as the wind dies with the end of the day, the sea is glassy and calm and only the gentle rise and fall of the ground-swell disturbs its otherwise smooth surface. Away from the island towards St Agnes the setting sun reveals a huge raft of black and white birds. More glide in on long narrow wings, their tips just skimming the sea. Soon, several hundred Manx shearwaters are paddling in the sunset. Manx shearwaters nest underground, mostly on remote islands like Annet. To avoid the unwelcome attentions of their biggest threat, the great black-backed gulls, they gather late in the day, some distance offshore, before visiting their burrows under the cover of dark. To stand on an isolated island far out in the Atlantic in the middle of a moonless night is quite an experience. But to be surrounded by beating wings and the eerie choking calls of these extraordinary birds is unforgettable, especially when the ground throbs with the same strangled noise coming from their burrows. Landing in the dark, often with a crash, the dazed birds gather themselves and each moves clumsily towards its mate calling from her burrow. The contrast of this ungainly shuffle with the birds' prowess in flight and their ability to dive and swim underwater could not be greater.

In addition to being well known for their ability to fly almost effortlessly over considerable distances at sea, Manx shearwaters are also renowned for their sense of direction. One bird, taken from its Welsh island home and released on the east coast of North America, some way from its normal range, returned to

Below: *Grey Atlantic seal and suckling pup. The milk from the cow seal is one of the richest in the animal world and this pup, just a few days old, will be weaned within three weeks.*

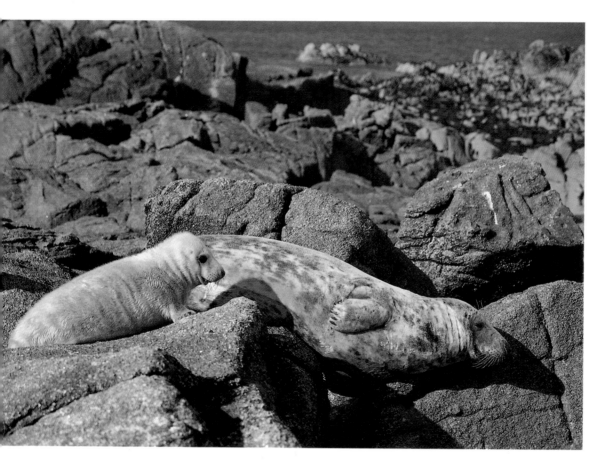

Right: *Unknown elsewhere in Britain, the continental lesser white-toothed shrew is renowned for its habit of 'caravanning'. This female has just led her young away from the nest in a line of nose to tail shrews.*

its mate in just twelve days. Each winter, Manx shearwaters head south, crossing the Atlantic and flying south of the equator to spend several months off the coast of South America. They return north to breed in the spring, arriving back at their nesting burrows any time from February onwards. Their faithfulness to a nest site is impressive. On the night I visited Annet one Manx shearwater found by the warden responsible for the colony had a ring on its leg. The number was later checked and revealed that the bird had originally been caught just a few metres away as a chick fifteen years before.

Breeding adults are usually at least five-year-old birds. A single, large egg is laid in the first week of May in a burrow dug in soft soil. Big eggs take longer to incubate and shearwaters take turns to sit on the nest for more than seven weeks before hatching occurs. Each adult's shift may last from one to four or more days. Development of the chick is an equally lengthy process as it grows fat on a rich diet of small fish. The parents feed far to the south, on the teeming shoals of sardines which gather in summer in the Bay of Biscay, and return from there with food for their young. Eventually, after about sixty days, the parents desert their now bloated offspring. In the safety of the burrow the young bird begins to moult its thick covering of soft down. Over the next fortnight it slowly begins to lose weight, revealing its fully formed feathers ready for flight. For several nights plump young birds may creep up to their burrow entrances, where they sit gazing at the stars and dim surroundings. Finally, in falling darkness, with a rising wind and driven by starvation, the young shearwaters emerge, shuffling out of their burrows into the cool salt air. When conditions are right hundreds may fledge across the island. The breeze tugs at the youngsters' outstretched wings ruffling their new feathers, then suddenly, without warning, a gust lifts the birds from the ground and they vanish in turn, flapping into the night.

Shearwaters are not the only nocturnal birds to breed on Annet. The storm petrel, another member of the tube nose family, is a bird of the open ocean and like the shearwater comes ashore only to breed. More graceful and more fragile in appearance than the shearwater, yet for all that a tough little bird, the storm petrel is not much longer, from the tip of its beak to the end of its tail, than a sparrow. Storm petrels survive the severest weather far from land, keeping to the troughs of huge Atlantic waves. Amazingly, they seldom alight on the sea, preferring to patter their tiny webbed feet on the surface while feeding on plankton, fish oil and offal. They are often seen following in the passage of ships, feasting on the propeller-churned wake. Their nests, like those of shearwaters, are built in burrows. But the petrel will also use deep clefts in rocks and even

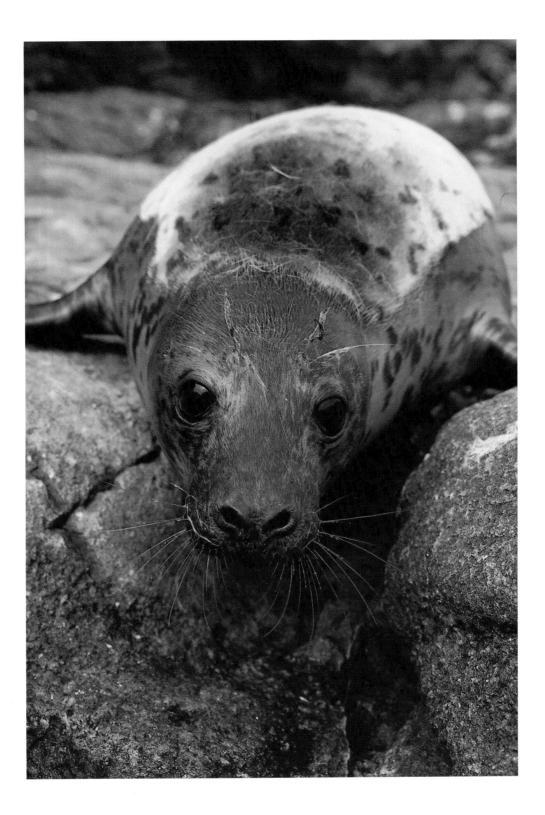

abandoned buildings as nest sites. On Annet the boulder shore, piled high with large, storm-thrown, rounded rocks, conceals a labyrinth of nooks and crannies. At night the holes are alive with the sounds of the birds' nocturnal crooning – a continuous purr to guide their mate home.

The single egg of the storm petrel is tiny, weighing just 7 grams, but it is a huge investment for the parent as it represents over a quarter of her own body weight. Even the shearwater's egg only weighs around one seventh of the parent's body. Storm petrels, like most seabirds, share the incubation of the egg, alternating every forty-eight or seventy-two hours for a total of forty-one days. The young is fed at first on a thick oily mixture, a pre-digested nourishing soup. Later, the load delivered straight to the youngster's throat is more identifiable: tiny fish, plankton and bits of small squid. At around one week old when the chick is covered in dense down and able to maintain its body warmth, both parents are free to forage. They devote the daylight hours to collecting enough for themselves and the hours of darkness to bringing the surplus home to feed their chick. At least one adult returns most nights to deliver its rich ration gleaned from the sea. By thirty-three days old the chick is usually as big as its parents, but it continues to put on weight for another seventeen days. After that its parents' visits become less frequent. By this stage, the adults are beginning to show signs of their parental labour. Their plumage is faded and worn, with feathers frayed and starting to moult. Finally, like the shearwater, the chick is ready to leave. Fully feathered, lean and fit, it will join the adults on their southward migration at the end of summer.

In marked contrast to the twilight upbringing and midnight flight of Manx shearwaters and storm petrels are the lives of much bigger birds. Cormorants live on remote islands along with the closely related and much more numerous shags. The Bishop Rock lighthouse is one of the most isolated outposts in Britain and said to be the most exposed position in the world. Work on its construction began in 1847, with the builders living in temporary summer shelter on the biggest of the Western Rocks not far away. Today the rocky storm-swept island of Rosevear island is inhabited solely by seabirds. Large boulders litter the rocks, and the remains of the original stone house is reduced to low walls in a wild garden of tree mallow. As if proof were needed of the sea's power, part of a ship's hull, wrecked and thrown on to the island, lies rusting here. But little goes to waste in nature – it has been commandeered by a family of shags.

The Isles of Scilly are certainly a sanctuary for many different birds, but the variety of mammals is much more limited. Lack of variety is more than made up for by numbers, however, and rabbits are everywhere. As elsewhere in

Britain, it is thought they were introduced in Norman times as a valuable source of fur and fresh meat. Their burrows and scattered excavations riddle many parts of the main islands and also some of the smaller eastern isles. In the past they thrived in the absence of ground-living predators, for the islands have no foxes, badgers, stoats or weasels, and buzzards are rare, making them safe from air attack. But the outbreak of myxomatosis in the islands has now greatly reduced the rabbit population. The fragile ecology of an island is easily ruined by introductions and with the decline of the rabbit there has been a change in the flora.

Another possible threat to the islands are hedgehogs, which have been thoughtlessly released. They appear harmless but are carnivorous, feasting on insects, snails and worms, and they are known occasionally to take small birds' eggs and chicks. Hedgehogs explore sand dunes and beaches in their amblings and so could represent a risk to ground-nesting ringed plovers and terns.

Closely related to the hedgehog, but very different in character and size, are shrews. The islands have only one species, the lesser white-toothed shrew, which is quite unlike the native red-toothed British shrew. Continental in origin and very similar to those found on Jersey, Sark and in France, it is distinguished by its clean teeth. Scilly shrews were first reported in Victorian times and it is possible that they were yet another stowaway on boats that traded in the past with France and the Channel Islands. They can be found almost everywhere – in hedgerows and banks, under bracken and especially along the boulder-strewn shores. Life is short for a shrew, probably not more than a year or two in the wild. The pace of life they lead appears breathless to us. An hour or so of frantic activity, finding food, eating, cleaning, investigating, shrieking and socialising, is followed by a similar period of rest, throughout the day and night. For such tiny creatures their appetites are huge. They must consume almost their own body weight every day just to stay alive and beetles, fly larvae and sandhoppers are eagerly demolished with their sharp little teeth. The shrew's face and tail bristle with stiff sensory hairs and these, together with its long, pointed, ever-twitching nose, signal the importance of touch and smell in its life.

Even the shrew's rate of reproduction is high. Three to four litters can be produced every year, each containing up to six young. Born blind and naked, the young quickly develop a thin coat of hair at around nine days old and their eyes open soon after. It is from about this age that a curious form of behaviour known as caravanning may on rare occasions be witnessed. It is an extraordinary scene to watch and one for which the Scilly shrew is justifiably famous. In what seems to be a response to a threat or disturbance to the nest, the female shrew dives inside and quickly reappears with her offspring, literally, in tow. The

Above: *The tranquil inner isles seen from St Helen's is in marked contrast to the exposed outer coast.*
Right: *The soft fur and appealing eyes of a week-old seal pup belie its set of sharp adult teeth.*

young, holding on by their teeth, are carried to safety. Sometimes they all cling on together, gripping the skin on their mother's back, half dragged, half carried. But more characteristically the young bite hold at the base of each other's tail, resulting in a train of shrews with the mother in the lead and the young trailing one behind the other.

Shrews are among the smallest mammals on earth, but some of the largest can also be seen around the islands occasionally. Cruising offshore, whales put in the odd appearance almost every year, but far more common are dolphins and porpoises. At times, huge schools of a hundred or more individuals pass in energetic undulations up through the Sound. Blessed with intelligence and a wonderful fluidity of movement, these extremely fast swimmers easily outpace all but the fastest boats. They belong to an ancient order of mammals, first evolved around fifty million years ago from land-dwelling creatures that took to exploiting the wealth of the sea. Several million years later another group of mammals, perhaps related to present-day otters or bears, followed the same course and they, too, adapted to a marine existence, although not as fully as the sea-going whale. This group, the seals, still retain their hind legs, which in the whales have evolved into a tail fluke, and their skeletons, particularly the skull, show many similarities to terrestrial carnivores. More significant is their tie with the land, which the whales deserted millions of years ago. Seals are unable to give birth at sea and so are forced to find suitable sites where they can safely produce their pups each year. The Isles of Scilly offer many such places.

At any one time there are around 250 grey Atlantic seals residing in the islands' waters. They seem to be in their element where the sea is at its roughest and battering the rocks, bobbing around in its swell and streaming white backwash. The males, or bulls, are much larger and are easily distinguished from the smaller cows by their heavy Roman-nosed muzzle. Grey seals can best be seen in summer, when they haul themselves on to rocks at high tide and allow the ebb to leave them high and dry. They are quite capable of moving over land but progress is slow and undignified as they drag their quivering bulk across the rocks. Front flippers, more suited to sliding easily through water, become ungainly legs, while their sparse mottled fur helps to protect the skin from abrasion.

Underwater, seals are different animals. If you enter their domain below the surface swell, in the subdued blue world of waving weeds, seals slip effortlessly in and out of sight, their curving bodies twisting and turning gracefully. The cumbersome animal that heaved itself across land now torpedoes past with amazing speed. The seal's fur serves a different purpose here, keeping a permanent layer of water close to its skin. In the same way as a wetsuit keeps a diver warm, the seal's warm water layer helps to reduce its heat loss. But the seal's real solution to the problem of insulation is its blubber, a thick layer of oily fat just under the skin that wraps the body in an efficient thermal coat.

The end of August finds the cows heavy with young, for the pups are born in September here. Groups of seals are usually separated into males and females at this time, with the large bulls patrolling the breeding or haul-out sites. Cows give birth to a single pup somewhere above the high-water mark on the rocky shore of one of the western isles. Delivery is fast, aided by the streamlined shape of the seal. From the first signs of labour to the moment of birth may be no more than fifteen minutes. At birth the pup is covered in dense creamy fur and its skin lies loosely in folds, but only for a short while. The pup is suckled every five to six hours on one of the richest milks in the animal world. Indeed, so nutritious is the feed that the pup takes its fill in only six minutes, although it may continue to suckle for longer. The cow tends her young for up to twenty-one days, but is ready to desert at the first hint of danger. However, the pups are not as helpless as they first seem. To humans, large black eyes and pale fur make them attractive, but it is an unwise person who attempts to touch a seal pup. Not only is it possible that human scent will disturb the cow on her return, but the pup has a full set of sharp adult teeth within days of being born, its milk teeth having been produced and reabsorbed while still inside the womb.

The pup's routine is a simple one, divided between eating and sleeping, and within three weeks it has more than trebled its birth weight. Now, instead of its appealing good looks, it takes on the appearance of an overweight furry barrel of fat. The cows desert their pups at this time, leaving them to fend for themselves. The bulls, who play no part in the pups' upbringing, wait offshore to catch the cows. Mating is now or never as the cows are receptive only at this time, yet gestation lasts about nine months, so how do seals give birth at the same time each year? The answer lies in the fertilised egg. Starting around fifteen days after the previous birth, the embryo of a baby seal grows slowly for ten days. Then, almost unbelievably, it stops. For 100 days development is suspended, before the embryo begins its normal growth for the remaining 240 days. Altogether, this gestation time adds up to one year, a vital adaptation enabling the seals to have the freedom of the seas.

Meanwhile, the pup left on its own moves inland as if reluctant to go to sea. If necessary, pups can swim from birth but the need now is to moult. White fur is rubbed off on rocks and floats in the tidal pools, now stagnant with the verdant bloom of summer algae. On warm days, or when excited, seals weep profusely, for unlike ourselves and other land mammals they lack tear ducts to drain away the fluid. By now the pup's mother will be far away, perhaps feeding for the first time in weeks. For a while the pup lives off the fat gained from its mother's milk, until eventually hunger drives it down to the water's edge. A freshening breeze and dark grey clouds promise heavy rain as the foaming edge of a wave races across the rocky shelf and washes around the young seal. Autumn gales will soon sweep the islands, washing the rocks clean with their great walls of crashing water. Lifting its head for one last look the young seal disappears into the waves. The last warm days of summer have passed, along with the cries of the gulls and the moaning calls of the grey seals. It may be years before the pup returns and several stormy months before its parents are seen lounging around on other rocks. Two-thirds of the world population of grey Atlantic seals live around the coast of Britain, and this is the southernmost tip of their breeding range. It is a sanctuary for the largest of our mammals, which are just one part of a remarkable community of plants and animals living at the very edge of the land. The Isles of Scilly, famed for their natural beauty and as a haven for wildlife, are truly isles apart.

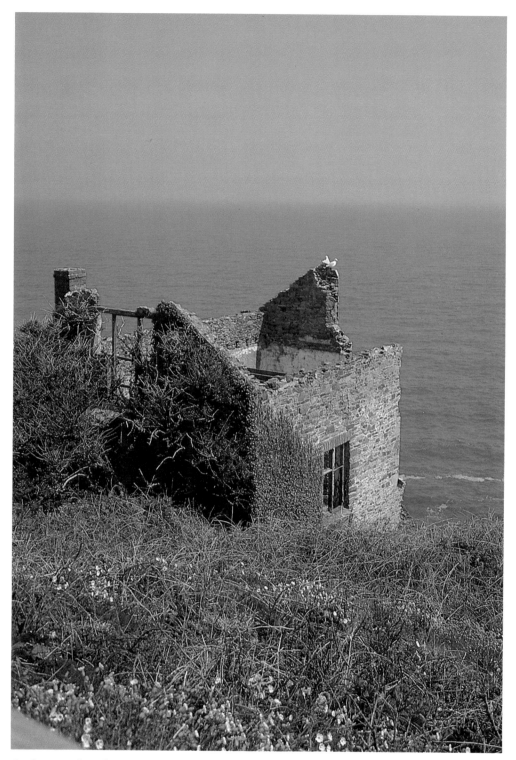

On the coast of South Devon the price paid for extracting thousands of tonnes of shingle just offshore, was the destruction of the fishing village of Hallsands.

CHAPTER SEVEN

Call of the Sea

W HEN DISASTER STRUCK a tiny fishing village on the coast of South Devon the war raging in Europe was entering its third year. The night of 26 January 1917 in the village of Hallsands serves as a reminder of the folly of interfering with the sea. The village was one of several small communities dotted along the coast that relied on the sea for its living. It supported 128 inhabitants before that fateful day, and was protected by a large pebble ridge. Darkness came early that afternoon as the pending storm blew down the Channel, a rare, strong, easterly wind. Well protected from the prevailing south-westerlies, the village became vulnerable as the wind swung around to the north-east and strengthened. The tide was exceptionally high that night and coupled with the fierce onshore winds the sea came pounding up the beach. It surged over the pebble ridge crashing across a wall into the houses beyond. Smashing through windows and bursting open doors, it flooded the ground floors of the houses, enveloping them in cold swirling water. One man dragged from his house in the torrent was nearly swept back through his own front entrance and only saved himself by clinging desperately to a door jamb. The destruction was unbelievable. By midnight four houses had gone. The inhabitants gathered the few belongings they could and assembled on the cliff tops above to watch the final blow. Even the dawn was not to relieve their anguish, for the following day brought another high tide and houses were felled one by one by the pounding waves. At the day's end only one house was left standing. The devastation was complete. Altogether some 29 homes had been taken along with the livelihoods and belongings of the entire village.

The greatest sadness was that this disaster need never have happened. Its origin lay in plans, unknown to local fishermen at the time, to extend the naval dockyard at Plymouth. The plans involved sand and gravel being taken from the seabed further up the coast. Dredging began in the spring of 1897 and during the next four years some 660 000 tonnes of material were removed. Activities were eventually stopped when opposition from several fishing villages grew as they saw their shingle beaches being relentlessly carried away. The first signs of damage in Hallsands came early in 1901, when the beach subsided by some 2 metres, undermining the sea wall. The following two winters then wreaked further havoc as the sea damaged several houses and washed part of the coast road away. By 1904 the level of the pebble ridge had fallen by around 4 metres, but with the sea wall repaired and houses rebuilt, life in the village was restored to normal. It was not to be for long, however.

It took eighteen years from the start of dredging to the final destruction of Hallsands village. It had been assumed that the removal of any shingle would be replaced naturally by more material that lay somewhere out in the Channel, but the high ridge which had protected the village for centuries, through spring tides and storms, had virtually gone by January 1917. We now know that the same shingle which protects the nearby villages of Beesands and Torcross at Slapton Ley was deposited thousands of years ago during the ice ages, and is not being replaced.

Today, a new village built higher up the cliff overlooks the scene of the disaster. The ruins of some of the buildings still stand as a reminder of man's meddling with the forces of nature. Now the inhabitants of these remaining walls are just the sea-tolerant plants that normally colonise cliffs. Their roots permeate the cracks gaining access to lime-rich mortar, which is an added bonus for plants that usually only grow in calcareous soil. Some seabirds are also quick to exploit the potential of such places. Wildlife is extraordinarily adaptable, taking advantage of any manmade structure or offerings. An obvious example is the spread of gulls: black-headed, black-back and herring all plunder dumped refuse, especially in winter. Herring gulls are real opportunists and to them the ledges provided by a tumbledown house are little different from those on a cliff, they may even provide more shelter. This habit of nesting on houses has also extended to newer buildings, still inhabited by people. The walls designed by some architects can offer pioneering nesters the same opportunities as cliff faces, so prospecting seabirds have no problems in finding suitable sites. Kittiwakes are already beginning to exploit some of these purpose-built coastal ledges. In seaside towns today nests are most commonly sited on the tops of high roofs wedged between chimney pots wherever possible, and sometimes even inside them. These nests, belonging to herring gulls, are a relatively new feature, for the popularity of such sites appears to have grown remarkably since around 1969.

The expansion of the fishing industry in the early 1900s seems to have benefited many seabirds, not least the herring gull, particularly around ports.

Since about 1925 their population in some areas has quadrupled. The great black-backed gull, too, has increased substantially in number. Although the subsequent decline in commercial operations in the north of Britain must have had an effect on them, both these gulls now frequent every seaside town. The success of the herring gull, which will eat almost anything, is particularly interesting. Through better management and recycling, the amount of human refuse available may well be declining, but the population of herring gulls is soaring. Their increase in numbers may not reflect the quantity of refuse available, so much as the possibility that they have not previously exploited this source of food to any extent and now do so.

Today, Brixham harbour contains one of the biggest fishing fleets in Britain. In summer, even before dawn, the place is a hive of activity. Sunrise sees the catches of freezing, ice-packed fish being hauled on to the quay in colourful plastic containers, then carried off and auctioned in the quayside sheds. Much of the catch will have been cleaned at sea, providing food for the ocean-going birds. Other birds, notably the gulls, wait impatiently on the surrounding rooftops and rigging. They swoop down on the remains of filleting in a screaming mob, quarrelling among themselves as each tries to seize as much as it can in the shortest possible time. Later in the season the adults that have learnt to scavenge from man are joined by a motley bunch of youngsters. Even the occasional kittiwake can be seen picking the odd scrap, but unlike the gulls the success of these shy birds is perhaps better explained by a change in their natural food.

The nets of trawlers provide more pickings for herring gulls, which have learnt to stroll around the decks keeping a watchful eye open. Whether the nets have just been hauled up for checking and repair, or heaped on board, the gulls still struggle to disentangle the remnants of the last catch. But some nets harvest more than just fish. The use of fine, monofilament drift nets that entangle birds has caused considerable concern worldwide and is now doing so in Britain. Birds were first spotted in catches in British waters in 1983. On 1 February 1988, two fishing boats off the south-west of England were seen to haul in five nets, which in addition to fish contained hundreds of dead seabirds. The majority of these were razorbills, with a few guillemots and two shags. The boats departed in mid-afternoon leaving a further net set, which already held many dead birds. Some, on the surface, were still alive but hopelessly entwined. Auks are most at risk as they begin to collect early in the breeding season when there is a greater likelihood of bad weather driving both fish and birds inshore.

The nets themselves are a simple curtain hung vertically from floats, with a

Left: *The high pebble ridge which had protected Hallsands village over the centuries dropped by some four metres in just eighteen years.* **Above:** *As hunters rather than farmers the fishing industry has far-reaching consequences for the nature of the seas.*

Below: *Sunrise over Brixham harbour reveals one of the biggest fishing fleets in Britain.*

weighted line along the bottom edge. They may be hundreds of metres long. In line with the notion that seabirds do not dive deeply, the net lies anchored some 10 metres underwater. It is ironic that the diving proficiency of many birds has only recently come to light due to the numbers of them caught in these deep-set nets. Reports that divers have seen guillemots 100 metres below the surface seem hardly credible, yet there has also been a sighting of a razorbill from a submarine. The latest deep-diving record comes from a guillemot trapped and killed an extraordinary 180 metres down. In areas where auks are already severely depleted, any further pressure could destroy the remaining southern colonies. And it is not just birds that are affected. Dead dolphins and seals are turning up around the mainland coasts and off islands, and increasing numbers are showing signs of being the victims of net entanglements.

So many modern materials are virtually indestructible and fishing nets are amongst the toughest. Where birds are concerned, death is not always from entanglement in fishing nets. Many seabirds collect flotsam along with the stems and fronds of weeds and cliff plants to build their nests. Shags often build their structures under an overhang or somewhere sheltered. The nest itself is an untidy heap of material which eventually, through trampling and fouling, is baked hard by the end of summer. On Menavaur, the remote seabird stack in the Isles of Scilly, a shag was found literally tied to its nest. Almost fledged, its parents were continuing to bring food even though the sibling with which it had shared its home for perhaps the past eight weeks had already flown. A length of fishing line had become inextricably tangled around one leg, causing a nasty swelling, and it took several minutes to carefully cut this away, a job which the bird had evidently not been able to do despite its sharp beak.

The discarded bits of nylon net and polypropylene rope which end up in nests are a major problem for many other birds beside shags. The extent of this waste can sometimes be astonishing and rescue operations are occasionally required on a similarly large scale. Every year in the wake of the gannets' rowdy and excited breeding season, a number of young birds, and occasionally adults, are found dead. The majority are trapped, ensnared by twining strands and fatally anchored to the nest or caught on the rocks. On Les Etac, the gannet colony just off Alderney, attempts are made periodically to clear the life-threatening debris. In the past, over seventy sacks of rope and netting have been removed at any one time with the help of the Royal Air Force. But such exercises are not without their hazards for the people involved. In 1987 the weather was so rough that a helicopter was struck by a huge wave and disabled when one of its engines failed. Luckily, it landed safely.

Seabirds also suffer from less obvious threats that perhaps involve factors we as yet know little about. Chemical poisoning and oil pollution are certainly among the factors controlling seabird populations, but the long-term contraction and expansion of a species over vast areas is likely to be related to changes in the world's oceans affecting the food supplies. Indeed, it was in the mid-1950s that this view was first suggested by the same expert who brought other factors to light. when Ronald Lockley visited Burhou island off Alderney, he examined many of the storm petrel nests, which could then still be found in reasonable numbers, and he discovered that the ground was swarming with red mites. Normally these tiny predators remain hidden by day and emerge only at night to suck the blood of birds. In a seething, hungry, red tide, the mites attack any warm-blooded creature, including man. Although only 1 millimetre in length, they can multiply rapidly in the warm weather of late summer. Many young puffins on Burhou were also found driven out of their burrows to die in the open from extreme irritation and loss of blood. It was estimated that several hundred young birds had been forced to leave the security of their homes, staggering, lean and weakened, to the surface. The mite appears to be incapable of surviving cold damp conditions and the warm southerly aspect of Burhou proved to be an ideal breeding ground. It is known to be a serious pest of chickens, so how did it arrive on Burhou? The answer will probably never be known, but it seems likely that the mites hitched a lift on the clothes of someone visiting the island in summer and so perhaps were inadvertently transferred from a poultry house on Alderney. The consequences were incalculable. Whether this was the major cause of the puffin and petrel decline, or just the fatal blow to a population already under pressure, can only ever be guessed at. When these colonies are so reduced, gulls, especially great black-backs, become an intolerable burden. For that reason many nature reserves now exercise control over the numbers of predatory gulls. Perhaps when the tide turns again in favour of petrels and auks, these outposts will return to their former glory as thriving seabird cities.

Man has not always lent wildlife such a helping hand. In origin humans are hunters, or to be more accurate hunter–gatherers. At sea, man is a major predator, a hunter and not a farmer, and is therefore very much part of its natural history. For millions of years people have reaped the harvest of the sea, at first around the coast then progressively pushing far beyond inshore waters. Even seabirds were considered good eating, and still are in some parts of the world. It is known that from the Stone Age they featured regularly in the diet of early peoples, along with fish, crabs and the contents of shells. The remains of bones and the huge piles of limpet shells found in the middens of ancient

settlements testify to the importance of the tidal crop, although I cannot help wondering if our early ancestors did not actually consume such vast quantities of leathery limpet flesh, but used them in some way as bait to trap fish. The fact that puffins were so highly prized in the Middle Ages as to be accepted as rent, also points to the past importance of these birds. Gannets, too, have a long history of being harvested, especially in the north.

The complex subtle ecology of the world's seas has produced an incredible variety of life, there are more than 6000 species of crustacea, around 11 000 species of fish and some 700 different types of squid. Where ocean currents converge, mixing, upwellings and eddies result in a vast, ever-changing pattern. Upwellings are especially rich but quickly exhausted. This is now clearly shown by satellites, which reveal an amazing scene developing in parts of the western Atlantic: an explosion of green phytoplankton growing up to ten times faster than in the surrounding area of ocean. But it seldom lasts more than a few days at that incredible rate. By then all the surface nutrients are used up and the bloom fades away. Coastal waters, wherever the sea is less than 180 metres in depth, have an importance out of all proportion to their size. Their productivity is at least twice that of the deep sea. As a feeding ground for marine animals and seabirds they are extremely important, yet in area they make up less than 10 per cent of the ocean's surface. We, too, benefit from these rich shallower waters, and major fisheries are based on continental shelves. Predators such as birds are thought to have little effect on the quantity and fecundity of this marine life, but humans have a far greater impact.

In the confined waters of the English Channel and in other similar seas, over-fishing has seriously depleted many stocks. Different species in turn have been fished until they begin to show signs of a population crash. Over the past two decades many fisheries in Britain have gradually failed as boats no longer came in with heavy holds. Vessels left tied up in ports for longer and longer periods, equipment not replaced and damage unrepaired all evidence this failure. Quays once hectic and heaving with trawlers now stand idle and empty.

Newlyn in Cornwall reversed this trend in the early 1970s with increasing catches of mackerel. Small four-man boats pulled in the catch by handline, fishing in a bobbing fleet more characteristic of native villages a continent away than a corner of Cornwall. In Mounts Bay, mackerel came boiling to the surface in a feeding frenzy and the catch grew to around a tonne for each man every day. Learning of this abundance big purse-seine trawlers arrived from elsewhere

Left: Although pollution and disease may account for some dolphin deaths, net entanglement is a major cause for concern.

Newlyn in Cornwall, a major fishing port, has seen its fortunes rise and fall with fish levels.

and quickly scooped the lot. The handliners then began to profit from another species, dogfish. Bigger boats again arrived and the glut went the way of the mackerel. By now some of the local fishermen were using larger vessels themselves, and so could venture further offshore. Since the mid-1980s hake have been trawled with increasing profits from the western approaches of the Channel. Each spring these waters seemed to replenish their stocks with a new generation of fish from which the boats could harvest a living. At first hake were found within a few miles of the coast, but by the beginning of the 1990s, fishermen were travelling out to the very edge of the continental shelf, more than 300 kilometres west of Land's End. Competition is fierce in these waters and nationalities clash as more and more boats chase fewer fish. In this political minefield the obvious loser is the sea, but ultimately it will be mankind. In one sense nothing changes and the Cornish fishermen are no strangers to restrictions, for in the seventeenth century they were limited to fishing no closer than 5 kilometres from the shore in a bid to save the dwindling pilchard shoals.

Other threats to marine life are not so easy to prove. Some may go undetected for months or even years. The use of metal-containing paints to protect the hulls of ships has a long history, originating from the discovery that a copper cladding proved an effective shield against marine growth. Paints containing the same ingredient in powdered form then took over as a cheaper alternative until the

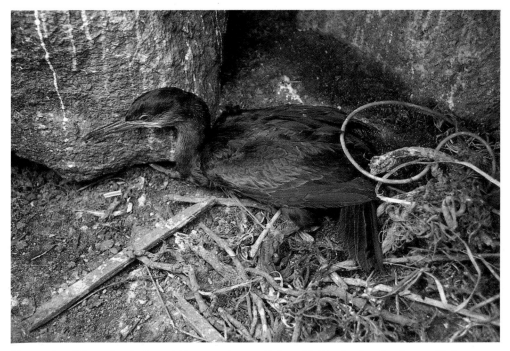

Above: *Its siblings already flown, this young shag, tied to its nest by fishing line, would have starved to death if it had not been cut free.*

Below: *Fishing has benefitted many birds, not least the adaptable scavenging herring gulls which pick the nets clean.*

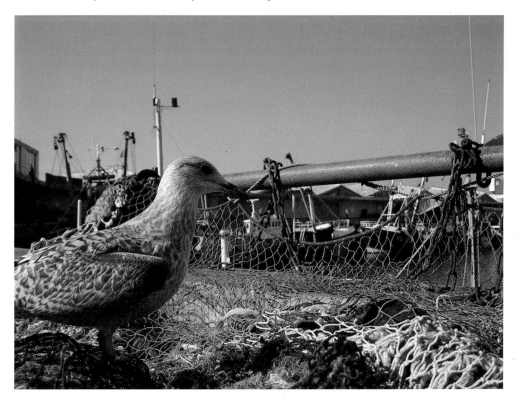

development of tin-based products in the 1950s. But the effectiveness of a new generation of paints became a major cause for concern. By their very nature, anti-fouling paints are highly toxic to marine life, their prime purpose being to prevent the build-up of marine organisms on the bottom of boats. The most successful toxic ingredient was a substance known as tributyltin or TBT. Unfortunately the poisonous properties of this chemical stretch far beyond the hull it is protecting. Even when diluted to an extraordinary degree its effect is still devastating, particularly as the larvae of most species are far more sensitive than the adults. In 1977 a French research team attempting to discover why shellfish size was decreasing, found their work led them to a harbour and tin-based anti-fouling paints. The problem was found to be worldwide. More investigations in the United States, followed up in south-west England, confirmed the fact that a creature that does boats no harm was being made to suffer. The dogwhelk is a common predator of other molluscs, especially mussels, limpets and barnacles. In 1986 TBT was found to have seriously affected it. Shell growth was malformed and surveys pointed to increasing concentrations of TBT in confined areas of water, in estuaries and marinas, and wherever anti-fouled boats gathered, as being the cause. As a result, dogwhelks began to disappear in many locations along more than 100 kilometres of the Channel coast. In the space of a couple of seasons they had virtually gone. But it is not just whelks. France was one of the first countries to impose a total ban after evidence linked it to massive failures in the oyster industry. Elsewhere, boat owners are keen to seek less toxic alternatives as TBT-containing paints are restricted in use.

The discovery that a simple whelk could signal the presence of potent poisons leaching into the sea is only part of the work being carried out by marine scientists all over the world. The challenge to seek new life and to explore the oceans and shores has been met by many people through the centuries. The year 1888 saw the opening of a new laboratory in Plymouth dedicated to education and research. Since then the Marine Biological Association has studied previously unknown depths and been at the forefront of man's thirst for knowledge. The building also includes an aquarium, which is open to the public and has introduced generations of visitors to the underwater world that hides just offshore. Rebuilt in 1958, refurbished and recently updated, it now plays an important part in education. Future plans are on a much bigger scale, with vast segments of the sea recreated in some of the largest aquaria yet to be seen in Britain.

Almost exactly a century after the association began, it merged in part with a national research establishment to form the Plymouth Marine Laboratories. Their aim is to unravel the complex processes of the sea, in a bid to understand man's impact on the marine environment. The work involved in studies ranges from mud-wading in estuaries to months aboard research ships and using the data from satellites. Subtle changes in atmosphere, weather and oceans could provide clues to changes in global temperature. The aquarium holds the evidence of warmer winters in Europe over the past few years in the form of a tiny seahorse scooped from Plymouth Sound in 1990 – the first to have been caught in the Channel for thirty years. Other exotic indicators of Britain's warmer water live in the aquarium's large tanks, including a trigger fish trapped in a lobster pot, a common stingray, puffer fish and a few electric rays. The closely monitored conditions also act as a temporary nursery for the occasional stranded juvenile turtles, until they are big enough to survive being released again further south.

The research continues, in many cases with added urgency as a new environmental hiccup is discovered. Plankton, some of the smallest living organisms are also the most abundant, occurring in the oceans in countless millions, and could dramatically influence the world's climate with far-reaching consequences. Quite how plankton work and what processes are involved, is one of the major areas of research. The fact that they are capable of moving carbon around the oceans on such a scale means that they can affect the levels of carbon dioxide in the atmosphere. Just how that alters in relation to global warming, induced by other greenhouse gases, is not yet fully understood. Plankton could help to save the planet or equally well destroy it. At the very least they could render the world useless for human survival. We do know that the oceans store around fifty times more carbon than the atmosphere, and that the sea and air exchange about fifteen times more carbon dioxide than human activities produce.

If we are to understand the ocean carbon cycle, the monitoring of plankton blooms is vital. Such work in the eastern Atlantic since 1948 showed a decline in the plankton population until 1980, since when the trend has reversed. In an attempt to track the progress of the bloom off Britain, scientists from Plymouth on board two research ships followed several marker buoys for a period of seven weeks from April until mid-June. But only as time passed did the enormity of the operation become apparent. Although the markers were dropped in a relatively quiet location, on the edge of a small eddy, they quickly dispersed in the currents. By the end of the study they had drifted more than 500 kilometres and spread out over an area of 260 000 square kilometres in the

Right: *Seen from underwater an oil slick threatens the life of the rock pool as the water-level drops.*

Below: *The consequences of a major oil spill end up on the beach, but cleaning can wreak more lasting damage than the slick itself.*

western Atlantic ocean. In addition, the products of planktonic growth also move vertically at around 100 metres a day. The result, according to the scientists, was akin to starting a project on a woodland in Norfolk and finding the trees had scattered themselves from Scotland to south-west England two months later, then discovering some of the leaves were already halfway to the stratosphere.

Pollution is a problem. Whether pumped, dumped or spilt accidentally, it comes in many guises. Sewage, both raw and partly treated, industrial wastes and heavy metals all contaminate the sea. As the scale of human activities increases so too do the effluents of modern society. Old habits die hard but the attitude of 'out of sight means out of mind' is now changing. When pollutants eventually find their way into the food chain, the insidious long-term effects can surface with disastrous consequences. Filthy water, too contaminated for safe swimming, results in dirty beaches. This affects the tourist trade, as people vote with their feet. In an effort to encourage councils and local communities to campaign for cleaner sands and seas, annual awards should give holiday-makers a clear signal. The cleanest beaches with the highest standard of facilities boast fluttering blue flags.

Mysterious deaths of marine animals sometimes reach epidemic proportions and the real cause is often difficult to prove. When thousands of seals began dying in European waters during 1988, pollution was first blamed for the tragedy. Tests subsequently showed the actual cause was a virus. But there is still a wave of opinion that suggests the seals' resistance to the infection was suppressed by chemical contamination. Around the shores of Britain, the grey Atlantic seal seems to have been least affected, while its common cousin has suffered the brunt of the disease.

There is one form of pollution, however, which is easy to pinpoint – oil. When the *Torrey Canyon* ran aground on the Seven Stones reef off Scilly in March 1967, the oil that spewed from the wreck created a disaster of huge proportions. It was the first of the major oil spills to contaminate the sea. In a desperate attempt to deal with the cargo of Kuwaiti crude oil the tanker was bombed and its load set alight. A pall of smoke rose from the stricken hull as she burnt, but not before some 121 000 tonnes of oil had floated away to contaminate the coasts of England and France. The most harrowing sight was the pathetic plight of seabirds, dying in a stranglehold of oil. A total of 7851 birds were recorded oiled in Cornwall in the aftermath of the spill. But it is now known that the clean-up operation wreaked more havoc. The damage caused by millions of litres of toxic dispersants drenching the rocks and beaches was immense. As a result, whole communities of intertidal plants and animals were completely wiped out.

Nearly eleven years later to the day another ship was wrecked, but this time across the other side of the Channel. On 16 March 1978, a supertanker rounded Ushant, the western-most tip of France, on her way to Lyme Bay, off Devon. The *Amoco Cadiz* was twice the size of the *Torrey Canyon*, and a disaster waiting to happen. She was carrying 223 500 tonnes of crude oil from Iran. That morning she was moving steadily through the rough seas of a south-westerly gale and was well clear of the coast when she turned to avoid another ship. Her rudder jammed full to port. Engines were stopped. The wind veered to the north-west and began pushing her mercilessly towards the Portsall rocks. Within four hours a towing hawser was rigged to a tugboat. In the meantime, the tanker had drifted 10 kilometres closer to the jagged, wave-torn coastline of Brittany. Despite the efforts of all involved the hawser broke and the tanker's engines were restarted. One of the ship's massive anchors even snapped its flukes as it failed to halt the relentless drift. A second steel hawser was at last secured just before 9 p.m., nearly twelve hours after the emergency began. Then disaster struck. Granite rocks tore the bottom from the hull and the ship was doomed. During the ensuing fortnight the gales pushed the ill-fated *Amoco Cadiz* harder on to the rocks. Virtually all the oil was washed away in the seething sea, to be carried on to the nearby beaches and along the coast.

In contrast to the chemical cleaning of Cornish shores employed in the wake of the *Torrey Canyon* spill, the French managed to remove over 25 000 tonnes of oil from the Breton beaches by manpower alone. They shovelled vast quantities into polythene-lined pits and covered them with sand. Even now it lies, a thick glutinous layer, a metre below the surface, like a geological stratum defining a disaster in time. Unfortunately, although burying oil hides it, it also slows the natural processes of decay. But the buried oil was only a part of the problem. The fate of the spill became a matter of international concern as researchers monitored its progress. To their surprise the oil seemed to be disappearing before their very eyes. During the first few months some 68 000 tonnes of oil simply evaporated, while around 10 000 tonnes were digested naturally by micro-organisms in the sea. Of the rest, some mixed thoroughly with the water, while over 18 000 tonnes sank and became incorporated into the sediments on the seabed. But that still left around 47 000 tonnes unaccounted for. It was assumed that some may have been broken down by the intense action of sunlight, but the remainder probably drifted away in surface slicks and tar balls. Nearly fifteen years later the sunken rusting hulk of the *Amoco Cadiz* lies gutted amid a growing profusion of marine algae and colourful anemones, and conger eels lurk in the dark recesses of her great structure. The tanks no longer ooze oil. In fact there is not a trace of oil to be seen. Now the vessel serves another purpose, along with hundreds of others that lie shattered on the rocks at the bottom of the sea. Vast steel caverns, portholes and passages form an artificial reef, teeming with a rich variety of marine life.

The lessons learnt from the handling of major oil pollution incidents go some way to help cope with any future spills, for despite advances in modern technology there is still one fallible element – man. The fact that on a bright, sunny day in a flat, calm sea ships with the latest equipment can still collide may seem incredible. Yet this happened. When Manchester United were scoring the equalising goal in the FA cup of 12 May 1990, the trawler *Dionne Marie* hit the 254 000 tonne supertanker *Rose Bay*. The collision spilt 1000 tonnes of crude Iranian oil, 22 kilometres south of Start Point. Within two and a half hours specially adapted aircraft had flown from their base in Coventry and were spraying dispersants over the slick. The oil now covered 200 square kilometres of sea, an area greater than the entire land mass of the Channel Islands combined, and enough to cover half the Isle of Wight. In terms of quantity, it was small scale when compared with the *Amoco Cadiz*. But this was summer. The seabird colonies at Berry Head were only a short distance away and the adjacent coastline is one of outstanding natural beauty, an area rich in isolated coves, weed-encrusted rocks and beautiful sandy bays. Perhaps more importantly for local people, the holiday season was about to begin.

During the next few days major efforts were made to disperse the oil while it was still at sea. But Wednesday morning dawned to a suffocating stench drifting up the Devonshire cliffs. The slick came ashore, splattered along a 24-kilometre stretch from Wembury in the west to Bolt Tail in the east. The thick, foul-smelling, glutinous oil smothered the rocks and beaches. The people living in the area were outraged at what they believed to be inadequate planning and a lack of response by the local councils, which resulted in a black tide being deposited on the shore. But this lack of action was born of practical knowledge. Attempting to collect the slick at low tide would have crushed and trampled creatures hiding in the sand. By leaving it to accumulate at high tide it could be scraped away with a shovel. The mistaken use of toxic detergents that left its mark on Cornish coves was not going to be made a second time. Even now, over twenty years later, the damage done in clearing the coast after the *Torrey Canyon* spill can still be seen. The fact is that if chemicals and high pressure hoses are used to blast the oil from every crevice, it kills the sheltering wildlife. Certain places along the Devon coast were worse hit by the *Rose Bay* oil than others.

In some coves the tar, thrown by the waves, speckled the cliffs several metres above the high-water line. The top of the intertidal zone was coated in a thick sticky layer, while a huge brown raft of frothy emulsified oil swilled slowly between the rocks.

In the most accessible places, where holiday beaches were spoilt, action was taken. The dispersant sprays available nowadays have a low level of toxicity and if they are used by experts with great care, and thoroughly mixed with the oil, the long-term damage to the environment is reduced. It is still very labour intensive and messy. The high power jet hoses hiss steam in great clouds, blasting the rocks in scalding bands. Brushing and scrubbing completes the sterilisation of the shore.

Up to now the remaining slick had been held against the shore by light southerly winds, but a change in the weather began to move it further down the coast. Wembury, an important wildlife area and a marine nature reserve, was now in the path of the oil. Here, a rocky reef stretches out towards the seabird colonies on the Great Mew Stone. Hundreds of cormorants, shags and herring gulls breed each summer on the island. The soft slate, deep pools, gullies and overhanging rocks of the shore are home to a multitude of marine life, and the great accumulations of seaweed rotting on the beach provide hunting grounds for creatures of the dry shore. Elsewhere on more popular holiday beaches these wave-thrown heaps are regularly cleared away. Wembury had much to lose from the approaching oil slick.

If left alone oil does indeed seem to disappear. The stench is the first sign of dispersal when the action of sunlight, agitating waves and devouring bacteria all combine in the natural processes of decay. On hot summer days slick-painted slopes facing the sun warm rapidly. The oil that hardened overnight gradually begins to move. Slowly at first, like some cooled volcanic lava flow, the black evil-smelling stream softens and begins to slump. Hugging the contours of the rocks, seeking out the steepest paths, it pours into the pools in rainbow-coloured swirls.

Offshore, in warm water, the oil's toxic volatile ingredients evaporate to leave a sluggish, chocolate mousse that eventually congeals and sinks. On shore the slick envelops the seaweed in a lethal coat, smothering sea anemones, limpets and topshells. At first these creatures simply withdraw on contact or clamp shut, just as they would if threatened by a predator or exposed by an ebbing tide. Eventually they may succumb along with the crabs that sought to bury themselves and the fish and shrimps trapped in the numerous rock pools. Remarkably, the damage done at Wembury was not as bad as first feared. Most

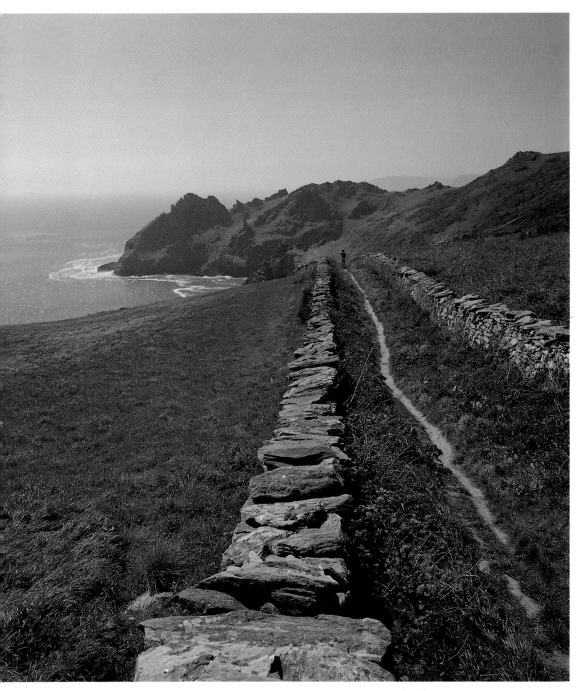

The coastal footpath at East Prawle in Devon, is just one part of the long-distance South West peninsula path that follows the edge of the English Channel in all its moods.

incredible was the lack of seabird casualties, helped by the fact that most of the auks were feeding much further away. The cost of the *Rose Bay* spill to the environment was sadly measured in a few oiled guillemots, ten cormorants and shags, and five kittiwakes. It could have been so much worse. The effect of oil on birds, apart from clogging the feathers, is to destroy the insulation value of the plumage, so killing the bird through chilling and stress. Less obvious but equally lethal is the oil actually swallowed as a bird frantically tries to clean and preen itself. One of the most vulnerable birds is the auk, since its practice of swimming long distances underwater means that it may surface in a slick.

The following summer the worst of the oil had gone from the most exposed places. Only where sunlight and waves could not penetrate did evidence still linger in tar-filled nooks and crannies. The absence of grazing animals gave the algae a head start as they began to colonise the bare shores. In the same way, on the Brittany coast, in the years after the wrecking of the *Amoco Cadiz*, the slaughter of the limpets and other creatures that graze the intertidal meadows produced an extravagant seaweed growth. For a short time the balance of nature was upset, with some strange bonuses. The local French fishermen in tar-streaked boats, brought in a bumper crop of the biggest shrimps they had ever seen. But it takes time for nature to do the dirty work, people are too impatient. Perhaps the real lesson to be learnt from these disasters is not how best to cope with oil slicks, but how to prevent accidental spillages happening in the future.

Among the most sensitive sites, easily spoilt by pollution, are the wide open flats and saltmarshes of the estuaries. Often the focus of human settlements and industry they are most at risk from the land-grabbing greed of reclamation. The first place to suffer from the dumping of dredged mud, refuse or other waste material is often the top of the marsh, where mature vegetation has become established. In terms of the variety of plants and animals this is the most valuable part of an estuary. The widening and deepening of channels can have serious consequences elsewhere, as the patterns of flow and depositing are irrevocably disrupted. Large scale digging for bait is equally ruinous. But even the presence of a lone digger, wildfowler or casual dog walker can seriously disturb thousands of roosting birds. The destruction of an estuary is sometimes more subtle. Shell fisheries, if not carefully controlled, can introduce unwanted aliens. Pests and diseases are the biggest problem in confined waters and the presence of oyster drills, slipper limpet, American clam or Japanese seaweed can ruin the livelihoods of both fishermen and the native wildlife.

The sheer volume of people flocking to the coast each year creates its own problems. One million people visit Dawlish Warren alone. Although the majority of them manage to co-exist with the local nature reserve, the wardens must remain ever vigilant for the minority who, through ignorance or malice, spoil the surroundings for others. Litter is one of the biggest problems, for beaches as well as city centres. At the least, it provides the evening meal for hundreds of scavenging gulls and at the worst, results in a child's badly cut foot after standing on a broken bottle.

The sun sinking to the west is the signal for the second big migration of the day, as people pack their bags and start to make their way home. Black-headed gulls descend in flocks to devour any remains, but they may find more than they bargained for. The plastic rings that hold four-packs of cans together are all too easily picked up by birds as they squabble over bits of food left in the sand. Plastic also floats, and any seabird unfortunate enough to surface under a ring could well find itself wearing a potentially lethal necklace. In an effort to rid itself of the collar, one of its feet is likely to become entangled. One-legged and half-strangled, starvation will kill this unfortunate bird in the end.

The future, however, could well bring an even greater threat. Global warming could mean rising sea levels worldwide. By how much and when are still the subject of great debate. The effect on the coastline of even a 1-metre rise would be to cause extensive flooding in many towns and cities if sea defences were breached. The lowest lying land would be most at risk, with saltmarshes being reclaimed as mudflats. The loss to agriculture would also be great as flood meadows become permanently drowned. In time, saltmarsh might extend far inland, to the benefit of wildlife and the detriment of the farmer. Perhaps even more important would be the severing of the south-west peninsula's rail link to the rest of the country. This line, one of the most picturesque in all of Britain, runs alongside the Exe estuary and sweeps past Dawlish Warren to hug the red sandstone cliffs. Here it plays hide-and-seek as it whistles through a series of tunnels to emerge sandwiched between tall gull-sprinkled cliffs and a sparkling blue sea. Each winter, even now, heavy seas break over the tracks, causing the cliffs to slump, and temporarily closing the line. A rise in sea level could undermine the already vulnerable sea wall, bringing all trains heading west beyond Exeter to a permanent halt.

The effect of even a small rise in sea level would be critical to the islands in the Channel, as well as elsewhere around the coast of Britain. In the Isles of Scilly, the main community on St Mary's actually sits on a sand bar slung between two taller chunks of land. Because of its position, a higher tide in Hugh Town could well be its last. But Scilly is no stranger to the long-term pulses of the sea as Nournour, one of the tiny Eastern Isles, first revealed in the summer of 1962. A Sunday boating party, out for a picnic, found an old stone wall exposed by recent spring storms. Excavations in subsequent years led to some of the most fascinating discoveries of the time. Within the confines of boulder-built homes, several rooms began to yield hidden treasure. Evidence of early megalithic occupation and thriving workshops was found in the form of small pots and intricate jewellery – figurines and nearly 300 brooches. This Romano-British settlement once nestled securely into the hill, with a safe anchorage lying beyond, at a time when the sea level was much lower than today and these isles were hills rising on land that linked the main islands together. In those long lost days the tide brought trading ships with goods for bartering. Now it just brings waves to lap at the door and threaten the crude stone walls. Some of the houses have already gone, swept away by the storms of the last millennia, while others now stand on the brink of the boulder-strewn shore.

Washing in from the Atlantic, these waters feed the life of the English Channel and the rest of the immensely varied coastline of Britain. Seas that support internationally significant numbers of gannets and grey seals hide more delicate forms of marine life along Britain's southern shores. Beneath the tidal waters, seaweed forests sway to and fro and herds of foraging snails roam the rocks, while streaming shoals of predatory fish and pulsating jellyfish swim in from the open ocean. The truly astonishing thing is that such a diversity of life can exist alongside the busiest waterway in the world. And despite the growing crowds of people that throng the seaside towns and squeeze into the harbours each summer, the shores remain relatively untamed if not untouched. The whole range of shorelines is here in the Channel, from mainland cliffs, both rugged and smooth, yawning bays with fine beaches backed by tall grass – tufted dunes, to beautiful uninhabited islands, treacherous rocks and isolated coves that seem a million miles from civilisation.

There is nothing more exhilarating than standing on a remote sea cliff, bathed in a warm salt breeze, listening to the call of the sea. The air vibrates to the incessant screeching of gathering guillemots, the maniacal cries of herring gulls, the screaming of terns and the cackling of courting fulmars. Birds are the visible evidence of the prolific life that coastal waters can support. They are capable of ranging further and faster across the oceans than any other creature, spanning the earth before returning to our shores. Together with the plants and other animals that fill every available coastline niche they play their part in the watery web of life. Tiny plankton and basking sharks, hermit crabs, herrings and human beings are all inextricably linked by the sea.